Sisters Touching and Agreeing

6/17/06

To My Friend Mattie :)

In The Lord Put your Trust!

Let your Soul Flee Like A Bird — Fly To THE Holy Mountain Of God! And Always Remember God Has NEED OF you! Your Strength Will Always be THE NAIL That will Hold PEACE Together :)

Olivia
'06

Sisters Touching and Agreeing

Olivia Thames

iUniverse, Inc.
New York Lincoln Shanghai

Sisters Touching and Agreeing

iUniverse, Inc.

For information address:
iUniverse, Inc.
2021 Pine Lake Road, Suite 100
Lincoln, NE 68512
www.iuniverse.com

ISBN: 0-595-28379-9 (pbk)
ISBN: 0-595-74792-2 (cloth)

Printed in the United States of America

To my parents James and Velma Keys.

To every sister, particularly those who feel they are unworthy to be used by God in a supernatural way because of failures and struggles. To Evangelist Delmarva Johnson, and Evangelist Lossie McCrorey.

To the Moses Ministry. And most of all to my very own natural sister Helen Johnson, you just don't know how much strength you have deposited in my life. Thank you for being you. Love you.

Contents

Acknowledgments

First to my Lord and Savior Jesus Christ, who is the author and finisher of my faith; I would like to thank my parents for all the times that they never once tried to stop me in all that I have ever tried to do. To my husband who I know prayed me through.

To my spiritual mother Evangelist Bertha Moses, for all the teaching and prayer life that has been deposited in me.

To my sons Jarkesh, Pierre, and Desmond thanks for all the unexpected hugs and kisses.

To my sister, God has truly blessed me to have a sister like you.

To my brothers thanks for all your brotherly protection.

Preface

For what ever reason I must tell my story. I must tell it for the same reason I had to go through it, I was delivered so therefore you too can be delivered. I have been healed and you can be healed also.

When I look back over my life my mind reflects back to when I was a little girl no matter what, I would always believe God would and could take care of anything. My faith was so strong it was as if I knew God personally. My parents surrounded us with love, but church was something we only did on special occasions. Therefore, the Grace of God gave me faith that I could believe in. But down through the years I would read my bible and become very excited about preaching, praying and telling people "don't worry God will provide". There were times in my life (early years) that I could just look at a person and words would just fall out of my mouth. And people would look at me as if I were crazy. But I know now it was God using me as a mouthpiece.

Through my years of walking with the Lord, I must say Pastor Benny Hinn blessed my soul. I read a lot of his books and listen to many of his teaching tapes. I love to listen to his tapes of worship, oh my God, you talk about being in a still place with the Lord, I encourage you to play some worship tapes while you are spending time with the Lord. My Lord! It was at one of his crusades that I had an encounter with God that I just can't explain. All I can say is I stepped into the rainbow. The Glory of the Lord was in that service, the color's were of the rainbow. I was inside the rainbow, that's the only way I can explain it. It felt like the sun was on my very nose! Oh my God! I will never forget it, never! It was so powerful, because I went to see God, not Pastor Benny. I had heard that if you ever go to one of his crusades, you'll never be the same, so I said to myself, WOW that means God is going to be there, and I went looking for God and I found a portion of him, a piece of his glory. I can go on and on about this experience. I must say he is a vessel that God is using to bless the saints of God. To God be all the Glory.

As the years moved on God blessed me with Dr. Juanita Bynum. I heard so much about this woman of God; however, I never sat under the sound of her voice, until August of 2002 at Women Weapons of Power in Florida. Oh my God! In that service I felt like I had "Twenty-Five" or more babies. I mean I was in Labor! Oh my God! All I can say is when the word was coming, I was chewing, and that meat was thick, and seasoned well. I was in a realm of God I have never touched, and again I went looking for God and again I found him!

I must say these two vessels really blessed me. I had a hunger for God, like never before. My sisters read on with an open heart and be blessed and encouraged. Remember the title Sisters Touching and Agreeing. No matter where you have been or what you have been through let go and let God.

Introduction

How often shall my sister sin against me and I forgive her?
Get your Bible, let's read Matthew 18:21

With the power of God moving like it's moving now, we sisters have no other choice but to touch and agree with one another. I believe God allowed my spirit man to travel from North to South and East to West just to feel the hidden pain, and see the hidden secrets that we sisters hide. I believe the information that you read in this book will bless, heal, and encourage you to expose the enemy. We can be changed in an instant, if we would just stand up and expose the devil. According to Matthew 18:20, "for where two or three are gathered together in my name, there am I in the midst of them".

Oh, how so many women are walking around smiling but their heart is broken. What about the sister that holds hate in her heart? Because jealousy has set in. What about the little girl, that has been trying to get out of that 30, 40, even 50 year old body? What about the sister of authority all that clout, first lady of the church, maybe a Pastor, but you're bound and tied up in secrets. I do not know why, but I know this is of God to release this book, and expose the enemy. We sisters will no longer backbite one another, we will be able to embrace with genuine love, we will support one another. It is time for female Pastors to stand up and say I will be the first; it is time for First Ladies to stand up and say I will be the first. It's time to say I will no longer live in my past, I may have been molested when I was a little girl, but I need to be delivered, I may have been raped but it's time I become whole again. "Hello" to my female Pastors, tell Pastor Betty Sue, I have been having these feelings of jealousy towards you for years. How about it sisters we must empty out the hidden secrets. I pray you will be able to release those secrets that are eating at you as a disease, let God heal you from deep within.

For where two or three are gathered together in my name, there am I in the midst of them

Matthew 18:20

Mixed Emotions

**Mixed Emotions
What are emotions?
Intense feelings (as of love, hate, or despair.)**

What about discouragement? Worried, lonely depressed, dissatisfied, condemned confused, tempted, angry or even rebellious. I believe it safe to say these are mixed emotions.

How many women are wrapped up in a secret place with mixed emotions? Scared to tell another about our problems. Oh how many women are out there in the world that really just don't know what to expect the very next minute. There are so many sisters who are living a secret life, and scared for their very life. The wife whose husband comes home day after day and beats upon her as if she was made to be his very own punching bag.

Everyday she is being physically abused and no one knows not even a soul, "my God". Then we have the sister who is torn down mentally, you're told that you are nothing, you're big, fat, ugly, stink, you are a nothing and no one will ever want you. What about the sister that is just not happy, your husband won't do anything with you, will not take you out to dinner, will not show you any kind of affection, you just feel empty. What about the sister who feels so low, you've been with every Joe Blow, you've been in jail, on drugs, on the streets, and living that life. What about the sister that lost her children? Don't give up my sister, oh I believe that if we women stand up and expose the enemy, we can become who God said we are. **(1Peter 2:9)** "We are a chosen generation, a royal priesthood, a holy nation, and a peculiar people".

How do we expose the enemy? By telling another sister. I'm fighting a lust demon and it's hard, I can't shake this thing, I'm dealing with a lesbian spirit and it won't leave me. Depression is overtaking me, all I do is get up go to work and back home and sit in a self pity atmosphere, I sit there and think of ways to kill myself. I don't feel love, the devil is tearing me down. I'm going through an abusive relationship and no one knows, I wear long sleeve cloths just to cover-up my body, from where I've been beaten. I wear heavy makeup to cover my tear marks. I deal with low self-esteem everyday of my life, just scared, always walking in fear. Sister girl, it's time to stand up and expose that devil now! No matter what you are going through, I believe we will all find a sister that is willing to touch and agree with you. Trust me, God will provide, and if nothing else, write me and I will pray with you and for you, because I have been there, maybe not where you are, but girlfriend I have been through some trials also. The enemy will flee in Jesus name! Remember our scripture, **Matthew 18:20**. (where two or three are gathered together in Jesus name he is in the midst of them.)

I remember a coworker of mine was in an abusive relationship and she kept this a secret for many years, but one day she opened up and we touched and agreed that God would intervene and God did just that, intervened. However, she had to expose the enemy in order for another sister to know what to pray for. I am reminded of my very best friend, oh how the enemy stripped her of everything. First our relationship, we were like sisters, you seen one you seen the other. However, she was always open to try anything and everything a least once. Me, Miss scary, no way! Smile, but always wanted to be in the midst of things.

Anyway, my girl started testing drugs in more ways than one. It went from marijuana, to drinking beer, to drinking liquor, to lacing her marijuana with cocaine, to snorting coke, to smoking crack. Oh, how the enemy set up shop in her mind, because all it takes is a thought and he can take over. She had lost it all. She had children and questioned who the father was of two of them. One child she had to give up because it was considered a crack baby, plus she was so far out there that she could not take care of her other children. She was not in her right mind to even think. The only thing that was on her mind was drugs, when, where and how to get some more. See she allowed the enemy to over take her life. Jail became her home and the whole time she was incarcerated she was still bound in her mind. She would write me and talk about everything except what she was facing, she refused to expose the enemy, the spirit of shame over took her. But sister girl let me say this, one day the Grace and Mercy of God opened her spirit man and loosed her, my girl is now out of both jail to man and jail to self, she is serving the Lord, off drugs, her family is united together, she is now a very happy, married, Christian Woman. To God be all the glory. Remember, "Sisters Touching and Agreeing". I said that to say this, if God can do it for one he can do it for another, "that's right" he can and will do it for you!

I remember there was a time in my life that depression wanted to overtake me. I remember sitting on my living room floor holding my head in my hands rocking back and forth. I literally felt my mind burn like a match to paper. You know when you strike a match to paper and the paper immediately crumbles, well that's how the enemy tried to take my mind, that quick he tried to take me out of here mentally.

But I knew in my spirit that I needed to get to the house of the Lord, I needed prayer and prayer warriors to touch and agree with me and that I did, my sisters in Christ prayed me through some things, oh how I remember, my niece was there, my mother was there, my sister was there, my spiritual sisters were there, and most of all my church family was there. See when the enemy comes in like a flood, the bible tells me **(Isaiah 59:19)** when the enemy shall come in like a flood, the spirit of the Lord shall lift up a standard against him. God will strengthen us to go through any door that the enemy opens up to us. See when the enemy tries to overtake you with the spirit of worrying then all we need to do is travel through the word of God, and stop on **(1Peter 5:7)** the word says to cast all our care upon (Jesus) him: for he careth for you. What about the lonely days? **(John 14:18)** tells us Jesus said I will not leave you comfortless: I will come to you. Remember we want to close every door to the enemy, so if we are dealing with anxiety, let it go, give it to God. If you are dealing with being lonely all by yourself, just know Jesus is as close as your breath. Let go of those spirits of confusion, anger, rebellion, discouragement, and most of all that pride, let it go now!

I remember there was a time in my life that I had to make a decision. I was very confused; wanting to follow flesh, not caring who else was hurting, and not caring what the outcome would be. But the spirit of the Lord said to me, I'll give you wisdom, read my word. I walked through the pages of James, and I stopped on **James 1:5** avenue, telling me If any man lack wisdom, let him ask of God, that giveth to all men (women) liberally, and upbraideth not; and it shall be given him. Sister to Sister, what ever you do, don't let the spirit of anger settle in your heart. See this spirit will weigh on you so heavy it will manifest and take total control of your life. All we need to do is repent and ask God to forgive us and then ask our brother or sister whoever it may be, to forgive us of our wrong doing towards them. Once we have done that we are free to go into the word of God and feed our spirit man, chew on thick meat, well done meat and seasoned well. The first piece of meat is **(James 1:19,20)** Wherefore my beloved brethren (sister), let every man (women) be swift to hear, slow to speak, slow to wrath: For the wrath of man worketh not the righteousness of God. How about eating **(Ephesians 4:26)** be ye angry, and sin not: let not the sun go down upon your wrath. This is saying don't go to bed with anger in your heart, forgive and ask for forgiveness. The last bite **(Ephesians 4:31,32)** Let all bitterness, and wrath, and anger, and clamor, and evil speaking, be put away from you, with all malice: and be ye kind one to another even as God for Christ sake has forgiven you. My sister I touch and agree that our heavenly father will remove all of your mixed emotions (any spirits) that are not of him. I pray for a hedge of protection around your mind, body, and soul. Remember this, there is nothing too hard for God. The more you sit at the feet of Jesus the more your flesh dies. Remember our scripture **Matthew 18:20**, where two or three are gathered together Jesus is in the midst of them. I am touching and agreeing with you my sister that God will restore and mend your broken heart and order your steps from this day forward. I pray that God will reconstruct you from the inside out, so that you may find you again. Get ready, deliverance and healing is getting ready to overtake you. Arise my sister.

Let's stay focused. Could it be our emotions are being pulled by a man? What about a relationship we know we should not be in? We feel all this is right because it feels right. First let me say this, if you are living a life outside of marriage (having sex) its wrong! I don't care how it feels! I don't care how glad the flesh is! It's wrong! Stop it now! What about an adulteress life? Are you having an affair outside of your marriage? God is not pleased. A relationship outside of marriage is committing adultery **(Read Exodus 20:14)** it's breaking one of the Ten Commandments. Yes this is under the Law of Moses, but **(Matthew 5:17)** tells us that Jesus came to fulfill the law not to destroy it. So my sister if you are living an adulteress life, you must stop it now!

Oh how there is so much we can talk about when it comes to our emotions, and how they go for a roller coaster ride from time to time. One day we are so high in love, so we think, we'll shack up with Joe Blow and know it's wrong but our feelings say go for it, we'll pay all the bills, knowing that Joe Blow is not working, don't want to work, and will not work. "Why should he?" Hey you're running things. Hello! What about him staying out all night, or not even coming home for days? Hey, he does it because you let him. Do you want him that bad, that he can pick and choose what days he will be with you? Because really that's what's he's doing, he is picking and choosing when to be with you and when not to. Come on sisters, we know the signs, and plus God gifted us with that special knowing feeling, the world calls it women intuition, but it's call a gift of discernment, and we know when home boy is doing something he has no business doing, don't we? But our feelings, will say, I don't care. We become so blind to the fact that the enemy is in control of the ride, he is in the driver seat of our emotions. And if we don't watch it the enemy will control every emotion within us. He'll drive us straight to hate avenue. And when he makes sharp turns, it's really hard to take hold of the wheel, because you'll be on an avenue that is hard to turn around and get off of. Once your heart has been ripped, broken or even cracked. The only sign you see is pay back, and on that avenue your heart becomes hardened and when that happens there is nothing anyone can tell you about what to do and what not to do. Because when home boy drains you dry of your emotions and plays you like you are nothing all you want to do is hate him and do everything in your power to make him feel the pain that you felt and even more. We start hating ourselves for letting him dog us out, if I can say it like that. Then we hate every man that even looks our way. We shut down on every man we meet. We close every door; we don't even want to see another man again. Because our heart is torn into pieces and lets face it sisters, if a sister girl heart is not operating right we can't function, just that simple. If we got a broken heart everybody knows it. Come on ladies we must feel right in our heart. So lets give it to God, and believe he can and will restore, and reconstruct your heart. He's the creator of every fiber in our body, we don't have to be led by our emotions, **(Acts 17:28)** says for in him (Jesus) we live, and move, and have our being. All we need to do is let it out, yes cry my sister, see because when we cry we are letting out the pain, the hurt, the loneliness, the low self esteem, the discouragements, suicidal thoughts, that's right come on cry, come on cry, that's right cry, let it out! Come on deliver yourself! Holler, if you have to, scream if you must, just let it out! My, my, my I feel it, I feel strength coming on, I feel a new sister being birthed.

God I thank you because now my sister is ready to pray another sister through. Now you are empty of self. See when that happens God can allow you to move on so you'll be able to minister to another sister who's going through the same thing that God just delivered you from. That's what it's all about, ministering to another sister. Remember the title of the book, Sister's Touching and Agreeing. I touch and agree with my sister that God will restore you back to a whole woman. Control your emotions one by one. And when your Boaz (Mr. Right) comes your spirit man will know it. Here we go sister girl, pray for that prayer partner God will send you a sister in Christ or will raise one up in the midst of you. Plus you can write me anytime. **Smile.** Let's move on down through the years. **Encourage yourself.** Remember when discouragement tries to sit in read the word of God. **John 14:1, II Corinthians 4:8,9, Philippians 1; 6, and Psalm 31:2.** When the spirit of worrying comes in read **1Peter 5:7,** and **Isaiah 26:3.** What ever you do don't let loneliness over take you, chew on Matthew **28:20, Isaiah 41:10** and **John 14:18.** Depression has no place in your life, cover yourself with **Psalm 34:17, 1Peter 4:12,13,** and **Romans 8:38,39.** And we will no longer be confused, and to know that we are not confused clove your mind with **1Corinthians 14:33 and 2Timothy 1:7** never bring the spirit of condemnations upon your self, the scriptures says in **Roman 8:1** There is therefore now no condemnation to them which are in Christ Jesus, who walk not after the flesh, but after the Spirit. And don't forget to read **2Corinthians 5:17.** If you ever get tempted by the enemy run as fast as you can to **Hebrews 2:18, 2Peter 2:9,** and **Romans 6:14.** We will not be angry, because we are killing the flesh with **James 1:19,20, Ephesians 4:26, Proverbs 15:1** and **Matthew 6:14.** Let's not get delivered and then become rebellious, let's stay on top of things, **1Peter 1:13,14** says Wherefore gird up the lions of your mind, be sober, and hope to the end for the grace that is to be brought unto you at the revelation of Jesus Christ; As obedient children not fashioning yourselves according to the former lusts in your ignorance. And we can't forget **Ephesians 5:8,** for ye were sometimes darkness, but now are ye light in the Lord: walk as children of light:

Do We Really Have Someone To Talk To?

What is talking?

To express in speech: utter words, speak; discuss, to influence or cause by talking, agreeing to use a language to communicate, to reveal confidential information, gossip.

I remember there was a time in my life that I would not talk at all, and there are still times that I will not say much, but under the presence of the Lord, that is a different story. "Smile", I remember my mother said when I was in grade school I was very shy and all I wanted to do was stay with her. She said I would just sit there in class and cry for her to come pick me up from school. No matter how hard the teacher would try to redirect me, in my mind, I wanted my Mother. I focused on wanting her to come pick me up from school. You see I was around people that I did not know. Well, that is how it could be in our growing up years. We feel if we do not know you, we cannot talk to you and definitely will not tell you any of our business. I don't care if it's life threatening even if I know I need to tell somebody I just can't I don't know you and that's all it is to that. However, you know that may be okay but we must know when to release something and when not to.

We find that there are some sisters, who definitely need to talk to someone and will not. All I really want to say my sisters is let us open up the lines of communications we must expose the enemy, we are living in an hour where we cannot hide. If we need help we must reach out, we cannot assume that somebody already knows, we must tell it and talk about it. If you have to go to your Pastor's wife, a coworker, call a prayer line, what ever you do just communicate. If you have a bible let's turn to **Nehemiah 1:6** let thine ear now be attentive, and thine eyes open, that thou mayest hear the prayer of thy servant, which I pray before thee now, day and night. First talk to God, and release this to him day and night and trust me some how some way he'll send a person that you can trust and be able to talk and release in confidence. Maybe you are a battered wife, maybe it is about your health, low self esteem, or maybe you are a self-centered person. Could you be a person that says my way or no way? That spirit can take strong control over a person's life, and it is hard to live like that, my way or no way. I know some people who are like that. If they do not have their way, they become very bitter and hate people. We find so many sisters, that are having problems with topics like, sex, drugs, friends, loneliness, how about just life, not knowing how to cope? Whatever it is all we need to do is first talk to our father, and God will intervene. I'm not going to spend a lot of time in this section, but I will give you some scriptures that helped me and trust me the word alone will lead you down the right avenue. Let us turn to **Psalm 4:1** "Hear me when I call, O God of my righteousness: thou hast enlarged me when I was in distress; have mercy upon me, and hear my prayer".

Psalm 4:3 "But know that the Lord hath set apart him that is godly for himself: The Lord will hear when I call unto him". **Psalm 10:17** "Lord, thou hast heard the desire of the humble: thou wilt prepare their heart, thou wilt cause thine ear to hear:"

Psalm 61:1 "Hear my cry, O God; attend unto my prayer.

Psalm 86:6 "Give ear, O Lord, unto my prayer; and attend to the voice of my supplications".

Psalm 55:17 "Evening, and morning, and at noon, will I pray, and cry aloud: and he shall hear my voice".

James 2:23 "and the scripture was fulfilled which saith, Abraham believed God, and it was imputed unto him for righteousness, and he was called the Friend of God".

So my sister as I said earlier I will not stay in this section long, so I will end it with saying this. God is as close as a whisper, as close as the air you are breathing and as quick as you can say Jesus he is there. Remember my sister put God first and he will order your steps second by second, day by day. Let go and let God, oh what a friend we have in Jesus.

I will say to the battered wife, use wisdom, get yourself and your children to safety and trust God. Go to your pastor or pastor's wife what ever you do don't be ashamed, it is not your fault, and trust me there are other women who have been there and will pray you through. Show your children much love, shower them with love every day. I know it's hard and it's not easy to love them when you are falling apart and feeling like killing yourself, but TRUST GOD, and I promise you He'll raise you up out of this. Remember Jesus loves you my sister and so do your sisters in Christ.

I Do

Do you take thee to be your lawful wedded husband?
I Do

To be happy all the days of my life, to smile every morning I wake up to my husband, to stay as humble and submissive as a wife ought to, to love and cherish until death do us part. "Oh, what words".

I once knew a sister who met this young man and only knew him about fourteen months or so, and before she knew it she was married to someone she really didn't know. During those early years of their marriage, they lived the partying life, every weekend, hanging, out and dealing with drugs and not really knowing that their marriage was not a marriage that God was please with. They had very different lifestyles. She was more of the low-key type of person, very much to herself and not very many girlfriends at all. He was more of a person look at me, look what I have. He likes to brag about what he have and really did not have anything. However the more they were on drugs the more this issue was not being notice. They could only make love with each other only if they were under the influence of some type of drug or alcohol. One day she notice that she did not enjoy being with her husband, not excited about kissing, or touching him. Something's wrong. She knew she did not know the man she married. How many sisters are out there in the world that is married to a person they do not know? Do not even know let alone love, faking it until you just cannot fake it any longer. I believe there are so many sisters that are living this way, trapped, and there is no way out. Well my sister all I can really say is this, be very honest to yourself first and then to your husband, and trust that God will stir up a new love. First it will start with the love of Christ and then that love is to stay until death do you part. Open up and really tell the truth. I believe your husband already knows and he will probably get a great release when you start talking about the situation. Let him know I do not feel you as my best friend. I cannot even talk to you as if a wife ought to be able to talk to her husband. There are so many nights that when we made love I just laid there not feeling anything, faking it and wanting it to be over with. Oh how we sisters go through the secret places and not a soul knows. Remember my sister we must speak about this and expose the enemy. After all, he is only out to destroy rob and kill. Well my sister I believe before anything can happen, like I said earlier we must be honest with self first, then with your husband, no matter what, we have to believe God can restore. I want to leave you with the word of God and let the word take root in your spirit and in your emotions and sit back and watch God move. He says in his word humble yourself under the mighty hand of God and he will exalt you in due time. Try to read these scripture on a daily basis. **Psalm 51:12** Restore unto me the joy of they salvation; and uphold me with thy free spirit. If we let go and let God, he can restore. No matter what kind of relationship God can restore, he can mend the broken hearted. He came to set the captive free. I speak to you my sister, as a woman of God; what ever you do, do not give up, let go and let God. **Luke 4:18** says this: The spirit of the Lord is upon me, because he hath anointed me to preach the gospel to the poor; he hath sent me to heal the broken-hearted, to preach deliverance to the captives, and recovering of sight to the blind, to set at liberty them that are bruised, to preach the acceptable year of the Lord.

Therefore, my sister I am talking to you, the battered wife. The sister who does not see her husband for days, and the sister whose husband is on drugs. The sister whose husband is in jail, the sister who feel so all alone, your husband don't ever tell you he loves you, oh how my heart goes out to you, hold your head up my sister, because God can restore and he's doing it as you read. God is the same God, yesterday, today and forever. Just as he said let there be light and it was light, he will say let there be life again in my daughter, and you will have a new breath of life. Remember God is the creator of your very soul. He was the one who placed the stars in the sky, and trust me he is the one who is in control of your life.

I pray oh God that my sister walks in righteousness all the days of her life, I pray oh Lord that you order my sister steps, day by day, minute by minute, second by second. Teach her oh Lord, how to pray, when to pray, and what to pray. The wife that cries out all night long because she's been beaten, the sister that has not seen her husband for days, the wife who husband is on drugs, father God strengthen my sister, encourage her to trust you like never before. I pray oh God that you stir up her spirit man, give her a hunger for your word and a cry for your presence. Build up her confidence oh Lord.

Let me share this, I was once asked this question, how much do a women have to give up to be happy? Why am I not happy in my marriage? Do I have to stay here? Sister, first I must say this, we must give up all of us. It starts with self-first, we must change our way of walking, we must walk totally with the Lord, and we cannot be Monday through Friday walking with the Lord, and come the weekend, be walking with the devil. Sell out to God! See when our minds are clear and our hearts are right before the Lord, then and only then will we hear from God. At that point those questions will be answered, it will be between you and God, just remember no matter what, keep your eyes on the Lord at all times, seek him in the dumbest questions and don't move until your hear from him. I will talk a little about this later on in the book, hey, I asked myself the very same questions, and God answered them all. Build yourself up my sister, here are some busters, **Philippians 4:13** "I can do all things through Christ which strengtheneth me". **Hebrew 13:6** "So that we may boldly say, The Lord is my helper and I will not fear what man shall do unto me". **Philippians 1:6** "Being confident of this very thing, that he which hath begun a good work in you will perform it until the day of Jesus Christ". **Habakkuk 3:19** "The Lord God is my strength, and he will make my feet like hinds feet, and he will make me to walk upon mine high places". **Roman 8:37** "In all these things, we are more then conquerors through him that loved us". Therefore, my sisters I just want to end this part of the book with believe God. Your day is coming, if you are waiting for Mr. right the only way you'll know he's the one is through your spirit, and trust me your spirit has to be in tune with the Lord in order for God to speak directly to you. Therefore, my single sisters make sure you are available only to God, and know you are special to the Lord. Being single you have no business being beaten, or abused in any way, it's bad enough that a married women have to go through it, but being single, that's uncalled for.

.

Being Sold Out

**Sold out meaning empty, nothing left: Oh,
how we sister ought to be empty of self.
Well how does this happen?**

With me, it started with all of my wrong doings-down through the years. First at the age of sixteen, I gave up the most precious part of myself to a young man that I was dating for some time. I am sure someone that is reading this book can relate, and will have a testimony to share with a young girl around the ages of 16 or so. I always believe that a woman consist of three parts, her mind, heart, and her body. Ladies, oh how I can go on and on about releasing our bodies as if we are passing out fruit. Let me just say this, I don't care how old you are, if you are not married and having sex you are living in sin. Do not be sold out for sex be sold out for God, do not give yourself up for the scarification of fleshly feelings.

Read Romans 12:1 "I beseech you therefore, brethren, by the mercies of God, that you present your bodies a living sacrifice, holy, acceptable unto God, which is your reasonable service".

Let us go over the years as little girls. Do you remember the years **(5years-10years)**? Well I remember most of those years; I was more of the tomboyish type if I may say so. I remember playing rough, climbing trees, and swinging from limb to limb. The only time a boy was on my mind or in my heart was when I was acting like one. I remember I had a boyfriend, but back then he was just that, a friend that was a boy. I remember him well, his name was Roy, he stayed down the street from my house. I could walk down to his house when ever I wanted to and he came to my house when ever he wanted to. All we wanted to do was play. See when we said we were each others boyfriend and girl-friend it was all talk, just word of mouth. I didn't care who he played with, I didn't care if he said hello to me or even come to see me, it really didn't matter, I just knew he was my boyfriend and that's all that mattered in those years. There was no touching, no kissing, no making sure I looked pretty, no smelling good, nor no dressing a certain way. I was just me and Roy was just Roy, children growing up. Hey there's nothing wrong with becoming as little children, for the bible **says Matthew 19:14** "suffer little children, and forbid them not, to come unto me: for of such is the kingdom of heaven".

Down through the years (10–15 years) I was more tomboyish then the years previous. I was into sports very heavy; I ran track, played b-ball, hung out at the YWCA and on some weekends stayed with my best friend. I do remember noticing boys and how they looked. At that time, those years, cute eyes, was the main thing, and a guy could play some b-ball or football. Those years we kind of hung around in groups, it would be a group of girls and a group of boys and all of us together were close within that gang. The guys were our boyfriends. Therefore, we all knew what the other might have been going through. If there was a family matter, bad report cards or somebody in the family sick, the group knew. Those were the years when you had a boyfriend but the most important thing was talking, we could talk about everything, we maybe would hold hands, kiss on the cheek and hug each other, but that was it, nothing else really mattered, we were being us. When it comes to God, can we really be us? Let us read **Psalm 42:2** "my soul thirsteth for God, for the living God: when shall I come and appear before God?" Let's take a look at **Isaiah 55:1** "everyone that thirsteth, come ye to the waters, and he that hath no money; come ye, buy, and eat; yea, come, buy wine and milk without money and without price". Therefore, sister I believe it is safe to say we can come to our Lord and our Savior as we are and allow him to clean us up. So when the scrip-ture says neither is there any creature that is not manifest in his sight; but all thing are naked and opened unto the eyes of him with whom we have to do. Seeing then that we have a great high priest, that is passed into the heavens, Jesus the Son of God, let us hold fast our profession for we have not a high priest which cannot be touched with the feelings of our infirmities; but was in all points tempted like as we are, yet without sin. Therefore, we can come as we are. "Let us therefore come boldly into the throne of grace that we may obtain mercy, and find grace to help in the time of need." Remember this scripture **Hebrew 4:13–16.**

Let us go down through the years, young women, these were the years when anything and everything happen. Oh, how I remember those years **15years-20.** The tomboyish look had to go, oh, I still played sports, but I made sure I was looking like a young woman when I was playing ball. No more big shirts and no more ponytails in my hair. I took my time getting dressed, and looked into the mirror before I left the house, making sure every hair was in place, my clothes were fitting me neatly and I was not going to act boyish anymore. Smile! Because the boys were no longer looking at me as if I was one of them. They would look at me and say things like hey cutie; your hair is pretty, and would just smile. And at that time I didn't know what was going on, but something changed, something was happening, and when that big year rolled around, sweet sixteen, I really changed.

I would hear older women including my mother, say, young women do not carry themselves around acting like boys. We keep our bodies clean everyday and neat looking, make sure your hair is clean, and combed, and you smell good, and always try to look pretty. There were times that we were allowed to wear a little lipstick but only on special occasion. Well my sister do you remember those years? I remember them all to well and will never forget them, I pray I'll be able to encourage a younger sister to really read through this part of the book and focus on what we can get out of it. But it didn't stop there, we were told how to sit, with our legs cross, button up your blouse, pull that dress down and walk with you head up. I learned this at the age of sixteen, and from then on, the experiences in life went from one experience to another.

I started dating, and was always involve with older men, and they were more mature than me or should I just say they had more experience than I did. How is it that men always would teach us how to really kiss? A peck would make us say wow, but when we learn how to French kiss, girl I knew I was in love, I went from a peck on the cheek to opening my mouth with an older man. What's going on here I thought, not knowing this was an open door for the enemy to take up residence and bring other spirits in with him. Oh, how they enter in. Let's look at **Matthew 12:45** "Then goeth he; and taketh with himself seven other spirits more wicked than himself, and they enter in and dwell there: and the last state of that man is worse then the first. Even so shall it be also unto this wicked generation". Hey, sister girl if you fall in this age group take these words very seriously because the enemy don't care about your age, all he wants is to destroy you completely.

I did just that, allowed the enemy to take up residence in my mind, soul and body. You see the French kissing went from kissing to foreplay to giving up my body, and if we just think back to the very first time we gave our bodies up, it was painful. Nothing was pleasant at all about that. We felt pain, and down through the years the pain traveled, oh the mistakes we made, some of us gave up our bodies and suffered for some time, but we realize okay I made a mistake, but I must move on. Some of us could not move on.

We felt the more I give it up the more I will get. How about we all know, Not So! The more of us that we give up the more we are losing our identity. Our self-esteem, our pride, our respect for ourselves, and our wholeness. All we really have to offer a man is our bodies, minds and our souls. I remember a time in my life I almost gave it all up. I was so in love no matter what, I did not care I was in love. I knew he was seeing another woman, but I didn't care. I still wanted to have the relationship with him. I would allow my mind to say thoughts like as long as he is treating me good it's okay. I would just meditate about being his wife, and what it would be like for him to come home to me and I will have dinner cooked and ready.

My mind was just out there, but that's how the enemy works, in our mind. I remember saying if I couldn't have him I think I'll die. How crazy that sounds to me now, but back then I was dead serious and sister girl if you are in that same boat, get out now while the water is only ankle deep and you can walk away. Remember those days? Maybe you did not go that far but I am sure a least ninety percent of you that are reading this book have. I said all that to say shut every door now, every window, every entrance way to your mind, because that's the enemy way in. He's out to destroy and his battle ground is the mind. Let us look at **Ephesians 4:27**. Neither gives place to the devil. It would do you good my sister to read the whole chapter 4 of Ephesians. I speak to the sister from the ages 5 to 20 years of age, that's right 5year old, you see the enemy don't have an age that he starts from, like I said all he needs is a entrance way, and at the age of 5 years if you've been molested he found his way in, because it was painful at that age also, the spirit of fear, was there, hurt, and anger. However, the enemy wants you to keep it all in, but my sweet heart you must tell it, you must expose the enemy, you must! That is where your deliverance is. It is all over now, let go and let God. Start today, your past is your past, your testimony will carry another sister through. Take the tears of Christ and the blood he shed and start washing your body down, start from the top wash your hair, for the word of God say in **Matthew 10:30** "that the very hairs of your head are all numbered". So wash my sister, wash it all out, for there has been some hands in your hair that did not belong so wash on. Now go to your face and wash away every tearstain, wash my sister wash. Now you can say what David said in **Psalm 17:15** "I will behold thy face in righteousness: I shall be satisfied when I awake, with thy likeness". You can start looking like our master. Now wash every body part all the way down to the very soles of your feet. That's right wash that rough part really good with the presence of God and as you are washing tell him God I thank you for your son Jesus, I thank you for shedding your blood just for me. I'm now washed in your blood and cleanse with your righteousness and I now give you my past, every pain, every secret, every doubt, every need, and every want, I give it to you. Order my steps from this day forward. Now say" Hallelujah I am free". That's right sister girl praise him, Hallelujah to God be all the glory. Girl I'm shouting with you thank you Jesus, I praise you for my sister, you go girl that's right praise him, my Lord, God is good, here you go high five smile. God I thank you, God I thank you my, my, my, something is happening in the spirit, God I thank you.

I have to move on, it is hard but I have to go down through the years. **20–25yrs** I will never forget these years, never! Never!

Those years for me was years of independence I was a single Mom, had a little strength to me and wanted something out of life, my own apartment, job and a car, I did get my own place and a job, which meant my own money. I was on Section Eight (Low income housing) so that allowed me to have extra money in my pocket. I loved to dress and still do, I guess that started at the age of 16, remember I wanted to look pretty, smile, anyway those years were fun and serious times. I was parting on weekends and was Mom during the week. What I mean is I couldn't really just hang out with the girls without taking my baby with me, so most of the time I didn't hang out, I stayed home, and I was having mixed feelings like what is going on why do I have this baby, I was mainly going through during these years. I traveled, I had family members in different parts of the world and I would just pick up and move, not very stable at all. However, I guess you can say I was having fun. Because really, I enjoyed myself. I met people from all over the world. However, during that time of my life I guess I was learning how to become a woman and a responsible one. So you see sister if you are around this age this is when we need to become responsible for our actions what ever they may be. Some of you may not have gone as far as I did and then again some may have went even farther. Whatever the case this is the year to really change. Repent, change your ways, ask God to come into your life and take full control, for he says in his word" we have not because we ask not", **(Matthew 7:7).** You know even when I was not walking right with the Lord I still would talk to him, I would talk to him like he was my best friend, because really he was always there to listen, I would talk not knowing the awesomeness of his presence. I really did not know him. So I encourage you my sister talk to the Lord and one day trust me he'll draw you so close to him. The more you spend time with him, oh my God the more you want to get closer and closer. Oh there is so much I could talk about in these years, I am sure we all been through some heavy stuff, maybe it is your turn now my sister just know it is all for your making. It is all to glorify God watch and see. Smile,

I remember my own apartment, I had it looking pretty and clean. Because hey you never know, you may have company (remember those days), or are you still living them? If you are my sister, start praying right now Father God give me strength to stop living a life of sin, stop the partying, stop the laying up, stop giving yourself to the world (devil). Stop now. Time is running out and the bible says "no one knows the day or the hour when the son of man is to come". **(Matthew 25:13)**. I know it's seems like hey I'm living the life, but let me tell you my sister. You are so far away from the life, and I say all of this to say I didn't just stop, I didn't cry out to God for help either, I didn't live right but that's why I'm writing about down through the years it took some years for me to realize that God has created me for a purpose, and that purpose was not to be a woman with babies laying up with every Tom, Dick, and Harry. Hey, if one wouldn't do right I would kick him to the curb and would have another one, come on my sister you know exactly what I am saying. So if you want out now just stop, there is no other way, yes, it will hurt but remember the very first pain go back to those years 15–20 remember we were talking about the very first time we gave up our bodies. It was not pleasant at all and the change of life will not be either, because once again something is tearing and now it's" our heart. But the word of God says "Jesus came to mend the broken hearted" **(Luke 4:18).** Therefore, my sisters get ready for a change in your life. The spirit of the Lord is upon me I must reiterate this again, the spirit of the Lord is upon me, because he hath anointed me to preach the gospel to the poor; he hath sent me to heal the broken-hearted, to preach deliverance to the captives, and recovering of sight to the blind, to set at liberty them that are bruised, to preach the acceptable year of the Lord. May I pray for you? Father God in the name of Jesus, I pray oh God, that you strengthen my sister and order her steps, remove every ungodly desire from her oh God. Holy spirit Teach her how to live a Righteous life. Everything oh God that you remove fill her back up with your glory, embrace her oh God with your presence. Sister girl get ready for a new day, your testimony will carry the next sister, trust me remember we are Sisters Touching and Agreeing.

Come on lets go down through the years. **Twenty five-thirty years** Wow there is so much I can say. Once again, I was traveling I went to North Carolina to visit my (best friend) here I am a single mom and still holding on to the strength that I had. My virginity was gone and my heart was torn, but there was some strength still in me to hold my head up and still look pretty and dress nice, smell good and all that good stuff. (So I thought) smile, I was in a strange land, around people I did not know (except my friend and family). I figure hey new town new men just maybe I will meet you know Who, (Mr. right) smile. You know we have to have Mr. Right. During those years, I decided to work and go to school, and I knew in between I would make time to party. I went out and started meeting different people and meeting new acquaintances. My friend's husband was in the military so I met many people in the Army. Different men, from all over the world, but they were merely associates, nothing more. Hey, I was enjoying myself and I was not looking for anything serious. I was enjoying the life of dating and plus I was not giving up my body and my heart was off limits. It kind of felt good telling your date thanks for dinner and I will call you. Not sure really what was happening. Was I scared? Yes I was, anyway, time went on, and I met this man who had all the characteristic of a true man and a gentleman spelled with capital letters. He opened the car door, took me out to dinner, surprise gifts just because, wow, money and goodies, at that time in my life I was a pot (marijuana) head, I smoked pot every day, and he made sure I had my goodies. Hey I guess that southern hospitality overtook me, smile, girl, let me tell you, a southern brother and city brothers are just the same, they just have a different style.

Needless to say this did not last too long. He was very controlling. Remember I still had my strength and that, I refuse to give up. Well I said that is it; I am not getting serious any more EVER. How many times have we said NEVER? Can't count can we? I know that's right! Anyway, while I was in that never land my parents bought a nightclub and wanted me to manage it. I met so many different people, Doctors, Lawyers and many professional men. It really felt good to be acquainted with professional people. As time went on, of course people wanted to know who I was, a strange woman in town running a night club, and single at that. I did meet someone who was single, who wanted to get to know me on a more friendly relationship, no sex, no body touching, really just friends. One I really became very close with and we would call each other brother and sister. You know it's funny because he was always there when ever I had those days of loneliness, special holidays, like Christmas, New Years, Birthdays and etc. I never really told him anything about my life, but some way and some how he was just there. He encouraged me as my heart was being mended and he didn't even know it. There was times I was in need of food, and he knew it, he would just come over with the groceries, he just knew. It's funny because, he was a very attractive man, dressed well smelled good, money in his pocket, and kept me smiling, but still my strength refuses to let go. He never really tried to start a relationship, why I do not know but it never happened, maybe because our conversations were always about other women in his life. We could talk for hours about anything and everything. He had women by the dozen. I thank God nothing happened between us because I would have been just another one on the list, and girl I'd been in the nut house, because I gave up my body my heart and all I had was my mind, remember I almost lost that back in the day.

Hey my sister I said all of this, to say until we confess our sins and ask God to come into our hearts, this life will follow us down through the years. We do things that we say we will never do. We will give up things that we should hold on to. Sometimes we'll say I don't care as long as he treat me good and home is being taking care of, he can do what he wants, but let me say this sister girl, first of all when we are fornicating, and living like a high class or low class woman, (women on the street) hello! Because no matter how we dress this thing up we are women of the street; there are sisters on the street and there are sisters in their own home selling themselves short. Remember this, it is a (life style) of sin, and it is not pleasing to the Lord. The bible says we are the temple of God. **First Corinthians 6:19** "Know ye not that your body is the temple of the Holy Ghost which is in you, which ye have of God, and ye are not your own?" Therefore, we must present our bodies a living sacrifice, holy, acceptable unto God. It all starts with confessing our sins, **Roman; 10:9–10** reads "that if thou shalt confess with thy mouth the Lord Jesus, and shalt believe in thine heart that God hath raised him from the dead, thou shalt be saved". For with the heart man believeth unto righteousness; and with the mouth, confession is made unto salvation. **First Peter 2:21** reads" for even hereunto were ye called: because Christ also suffered for us, leaving us an example, that ye should follow his steps". Walk right into **Ephesians chapter 4 starting at 22 verse,** "That ye put off concerning the former conversation the old man, which is corrupt according to the deceitful lust; and be renewed in the spirit of your mind; and that ye put on the new man, which after God is created in righteousness and true holiness." Hey, he will even give you a clean heart, read **Psalm 51:10** create in me a clean heart, O God; and renew a right spirit within me. My sister there comes a time in our lives that we must see ourselves for who we really are. There are sisters who do not have the strength to stand on their own two feet. "Just got to have a man." Don't care what he looks like, not saying looks are everything but come on now, he has to almost look like a man of class, some kind of style to him. What about a brother that doesn't even have a job? We don't care as long as he comes to see me, hey working the streets is fine because, if he beats the street that's quick money for me, that's clothes on my back, hey that's a hair do, my nails done, and wining and dining. As long as that is being done, I am okay. But sister girl let me say this, a real woman will say, as long as I got Jesus I can stand, because he's all I need. The bible say's he will give me the desire of my heart, and the hair do's, fake nails and the name brands are just that, desire's. Read **(John 15:7)** if you abide in me and my words abide in you, ye shall ask what ye will, and it shall be done unto you.

So my sister, after we repent and confess, and let the word of God come into our lives, all we need to do is ask Our Father to order our steps and watch, a new you will come forth. No more weak sisters needing a man just to say I got a man. No more weak sisters sleeping with Joe Blow tonight knowing that he's creeping out in the wee hours to go home to his other half. No more weak sisters selling herself short for a quick dollar. No more weak sister wanting another woman because a man has hurt her just that bad, that she feel she needs another woman, come on girl, say to yourself, I'm too much woman. That' right, call that woman out of you, she's in there way down deep, trust me she's in there! God created you all woman and that's what you need to stand up as, a whole woman. WOMAN come forth! Thank you Jesus, Glory Hallelujah, glory to your holy name. My sister let's touch and agree, Father God, in the name of Jesus, we ask oh Lord that you remove any and everything that is not of you; take away every weak spirit, that has controlled me down through the years, every thought that has controlled me, saying I'm nothing, will never be nothing and if I don't have it now I'll never get it. Sister you are in my prayers and know this you have a prayer partner, me. Sister let me say this I believe we can never go so low, that God cannot pick us up. I don't care how short your arm is, raise it up that's right lift it up now take a grip, that's right, hold on to God's unchanging hand, because he never changes never! He was there for the worst of them and he will be there for you. Just hold on because a change is coming. I know because God has pull me through many of fires and I did not get burn, I may not be where you are and maybe not where you have been, but trust me I been through some things. My God, hallelujah glory be to God. Let us go we have some more traveling to do, down through the years.

Thirty-forty years—these were the years, if I can say this, it was a roller coaster ride. Remember when we were younger and went to the carnivals and rode the roller coasters, well this was one of my favorite rides. It would start off slow then we would go up very high and look down at the people and all the lights, it was so pretty looking around at all the lights and glitter. In addition, it felt like hey I am way up here everybody look at me, if you think about it 90% of the people do look up to watch those that are on the roller coaster ride. Anyway when you are up that high you can see it all. Nothing can go pass you, without you seeing it, well that's how I felt during these years because I got past the years of needing a man, I got past the years of wanting a man, and I really got past the years of placing bricks around my life, because down through the years that's what I did, place bricks until I built a wall around me. I got pass all of that and I was looking down and saw Mr. right, so here goes the ride down fast I came hands up, smiling, and screaming, I did it I got married, before I hit 40. Hello! They will not catch me 40 and single. Girlfriend I did it! I tied the knot, as the world would say. These years (I was 32 when I got married), I was still running the Night Club, still independent very much so, and a woman in charge of herself. Had my own car, own business, own house, own money and was able to tease the brothers, because I was married and it was off limits to them. Hey it was kind of like playing with their minds, and their emotions, because hey they did it to me.

What goes around comes around I thought to myself. Girl I was in love, had a husband that was dressing like a city brother, you know I am a city girl, and there was nothing like a city brother at that time in my life. He was smelling good and looking good, and had a very good job. We both were making it and having fun. For about three years we were living the life, partying and hanging out but after those years went by something happen to me, my life was changed, I became a mother again, at age 35, and I picked up some weigh and I became big. I didn't feel pretty anymore and there went my self esteem. I was not use to this at all, I did not party anymore, and I stayed home all the time. My husband he still was partying and running the streets. I had no desire at all for nothing. My life changed, one day in 1993 my mother had to have heart surgery I was living in North Carolina and she was in Philadelphia which meant I was hours away from her, there was nothing I could do at that very moment, so I cried out to God like never before, and I said to him, if you would spare my mothers life you could have mine. Not knowing what I was saying all I knew is that my mother needed the hand of God upon her life. I was making a commitment to God and did not really know it, but I confess to you now my covenant with the Lord is still locked under that Covenant. I have been walking with the Lord every since. Yes, there has been times in my life that saints have witnessed to me, but that wasn't my timing, but I thank God for keeping me until he called me in.

Now I am on the other side walking boldly as a righteous holy woman of God. I said all this to say no matter our life style, down through the years it will come a time in our life that everything will stop. Sooner or later, bright lights will become dim, fine clothes will become rags, the up to date hair do's will become hats or ponytails, the smell of good perfume you will wear every now and then. One day nothing will matter, only you and God, and when he steps into your life it really don't matter, He is all you need. When my life changed oh how I prayed my husband to come over to the other side with me. I prayed and I prayed, but no change. During my waiting time the enemy crept in and we had to separate, but you know those are really the years that I was sold out to God. My husband would say things and do things that was making the old me come back to life, I started laying bricks again, I stacked and I stacked, you know the more I stacked one, 5 or 6 of them would fall down, God would not allowed them to stay up. He made me deal with the situation, and that's when I really found out who I was. I dealt with those past hurts instead of placing brinks on top of it. There were times in my life I thought I was not a good mother, because of the lifestyle that my oldest son chose to live. I felt empty to self. But God had me look the devil eyeball to eyeball and say Satan get thee behind me now! My past is over I'm washed with the blood, and no weapon that is form against me shall prosper, see this scripture in **Isaiah 54:17**. Girl there is nothing like the word of God to heal you, to set you free and to deliver you. Hallelujah, my Lord glory, glory, glory, thank you Jesus thank you, Hallelujah, Hallelujah, my God I got to praise him, my, my, my. Sister I started washing myself with the word of God. I stayed in the word for hours. God would wake me up around one, two three, even four in the morning, and I would get up and go to the word. I was being healed, delivered, set free, mold and shaped into the woman God wanted me to be. My flesh was dying and I thank God, because Miss independent would show up cussing, and fusing and had the nerve to say I was saved. Girl I was a hot mess when I first turn my life over to the Lord. I thought because I stop the life style everything else would change but it did not work like that, I had to change, that's right we have to do our part. We must start and God will direct. In addition, that is what he did; order my steps into the direction I am in now. I have been saved now for almost 10yrs, and I would not turn back for no one and I am not trying to miss God in nothing. Girl there is no other life. If I want to wear the finest of clothes, God has bless me with them. If I want to smell good, God has blessed me with the top of the line perfumes. If I want to have that hair do every day, guess what I am a Licensed Beauticians. My God Jesus, the fine jewelry, guess what God has bless me with a good job working with a jewelry company. Rubies, diamonds, and pearls, you name it if I wanted it it's mines for the asking, God blessed me with them. Remember we are agreeing with one another, if he can do it for me, I know he will do it for you. I feel like shouting, girl you just do not know, my God hallelujah, praise God. I went through some things. Sister, I just want to end this section saying all the trials, all the pain, all the tears all the lonely hours, all the hidden secrets all the why me, equips you for being sold out for God. Say to yourself, say it to another sister, I went through something, I was knockdown but hey I'm back up standing on two feet, my own feet. So now my sister put one foot in front of the other and start walking. Walk away from Joe Blow, if your living with him, you are living in sin, that's right walk, keep walking, now turn on to repentance blvd.

Roman 10:9,10 That if thou shalt confess with thy mouth the Lord Jesus, and shalt believe in thine heart that God hath raised him from the dead, thou shalt be saved, for with the heart man believeth unto righteousness; and with the mouth confession is made unto salvation. Now that you have confessed all things to the lord, you can walk down **Isaiah 43:25** I,even I, am he that blotteth out they transgressions for mine own sake, and will not remember thy sins. You are on Forgiveness Avenue. God remembers no more. So now you can start all over, become a virgin again, and wait on your Boaz. How do we wait? You wait by allowing God to change you starting with your mind and your heart at the same time. Renew your mind, because that is where the enemy starts that is his battleground. That way if your mind is cover then your heart will not be filled up with those mixed emotions, remember section one. If we can do this, then everything will fall in place, the woman of righteousness will come forth, the holiness of God will over take you, and you will be glowing with out wearing makeup. Because the glory of God will be upon you. When we let go and let

God, He changes every thing. Our garments become the fruits of the spirits. Lets turn to **Galatians 5:22**, the fruit of the spirit is love, joy, peace, long-suffering, gentleness, goodness, faith, meekness, and temperance. So my sister you will have joy in the morning, no more hang over. He will remove the garment of heaviness and put on the garment of praise. That's right the garment of praise, it's in the word of God, turn to **Isaiah 61:3** To appoint unto them that mourn in Zion, to give unto them beauty for ashes, the oil of joy for mourning, the garment of praise for the sprit of heaviness; that they might be call trees of righteousness the planting of the lord, than he might be glorified. Are you ready? Sure, you are because you are now covered with the blood.

Section five will be words of encouragement because we all need to know if God can't do it, it can't be done. I pray that some way and some how this book will minister to you, and that God will be glorified, if you feel led encourage another sister to read this book. Know God hands are upon your life, no matter what.

Strength nuggets
Luke 10:19 Behold, I give unto you power to tread on serpents and scorpions, and over all the power of the enemy: and nothing shall by any means hurt you.

Mark 16: 18 They shall take up serpents; and if they drink any deadly thing, it shall not hurt them; they shall lay hands on the sick and they shall recover.

Psalm 91: 13 thou shalt tread upon the lion and adder: the young lion and the dragon shalt thou trample under feet.

John 8:44 Satan you are a liar and the father of lies.

Romans 8:38–39 For I'm persuaded, that neither death, nor life, nor angels, nor principalities, nor powers, nor things present, nor things to come, Nor height, nor depth, nor any other creature, shall be able to separate us from the love of God, which is in Christ Jesus our Lord.

If God Can't Do It, It Can't Be Done.

If God cannot do it, it cannot be done

Well my sister, How powerful this title is. Because during these years, 40–50, if God did not do it, if he did not intervene when he did only he knows where and what I would be doing with my life.

See it was when I was 40 that I was separated from my husband. My heart was torn into pieces. I was unhappy, and my self esteem was lower than low. I gained weight, oh my God; I went from a size 11/12 to size 22. Girl I was messed up mentally and physically.

I had to deal with what it was like to have low self-esteem; I never ever had to deal with that in my life, Because I was always a very independent person and had very high confidence in myself.

Remember, in section 4, Miss Independent? That's why I really could not handle it; I could not cope at all. However, it was an issue I had to deal with. This is the reason why I can say if God cannot do it, it can't be done. It took God to show me, who I was. I stopped loving myself, I hated myself and nothing matter. However, I thank God for allowing me to find me again and to love myself all over. Oh my God, as soon as he allowed that to happen, I became concerned about my eating habits, and my general health. I was focusing on how out of shape I was and what I needed to do first for my health. My attitudes changed from the worst to a loving kind person that I use to be. I started dressing like I use to dress, and I was looking like myself, able to hold my head up and walking proud. I would keep a smile on my face, because I found me again, and it really felt good. Therefore, my sisters if you are in this place, seek the face of God, and ask him to heal you from the inside out. I started encouraging myself, saying girl you look good today. As time went on I was even feeling myself come alive, and alive and alive, and by then, I was standing on two feet looking in the mirror saying how you like me now. "Smile".

That was on the outside, inside I was still heavy, carrying around weight, I asked God to do a work in me, and sister when I asked him that, oh my God, this thing is not easy, but if we let God do it in us, he'll give us the strength to receive what he is laying before us. Oh how he showed me selfishness, pride, "big time" self centered person, and he showed me how my independence was only there because I didn't want to face life, I didn't want to deal with everyday problems. You see if I kept people at a distance then there was no way I could ever get hurt. Oh how true this was. But to God be all the glory, if he didn't do it, it could not have been done, I no longer walk in pride anymore, I'm no longer surrounded by selfishness, pride can no longer control me, and the spirit of independence is gone. I depend on no one but God. You see the separation kept me on my knees, in the word and seeking his face to do it in me, clean me up oh Lord, do it in me, no one but me, I was about me being cleaned up before the Lord. My prayer always was anything that is not of you oh Lord take it out. Everyday that was my prayer, kill the flesh oh God. I felt like Paul, I was and wanted to die daily. To God be all the glory, remember let go and let God and it can be done. My walk with the Lord became my first priority. I put God first in everything. I had to give up some things in order to get some things. I gave up self in order to get the fullness of God. As I was being healed from all the hurt and pain, I was able to hear the voice of God very clearly. See He strengthened me to go back home to my husband, this was not easy at all, but this only came after I allowed myself to look in the mirror and see me. Now mind you, all of me was not dead and trust me it was not easy to go back and I was still dying.

However, I put God first, it did not matter I wanted to walk in the obedience of the Lord. Nevertheless, the very day I went home walls started coming down. I was able to embrace my husband; I was able to say I am sorry even though I felt 90% of the separation was his fault. When I notice the walls coming down, I realize that God has done surgery on my heart. Oh my God, yes he did! Because my heart, was as hard as a brick. oh how he removed the blockage. You know how they say your arteries become clogged because plaque becomes thick and the blood can't flow, well that's how my heart was. The blood of Jesus could not flow in my life correctly because my heart was clogged with mess, but God removed and unclogged my mess. My Lord, hate was remove, I really hated my husband. I could not even look at him; I hated him just that much. I felt, out of all people, my husband tearing my heart apart; I hated him I could not stand to look at him. See when that happen my entire past came back to life. I thought all of that was behind me, but it all came back full force, I didn't care how much he was hurting, I wanted his heart to be ripped out, because for one thing I shouldn't have married him. You know how we do, start finding fault in the other person, so I had all these reason why I wanted his heart broken and torn into pieces. Nevertheless, God removed all of that instantly! As if I never felt those feelings at all.

How amazing our God is. Sister let me tell you if God cannot do it, it can't be done. Trust me I felt like I never left. The peace of God was there. During the years that I was gone, my husband turned his life over to the Lord. I'm reminded how many times I prayed for him to come to church with me and just be a family that would stay together in the Lord. I prayed and prayed and prayed, and nothing happened, so I thought, because I did not see it in the natural, but let me say this, when we send up a prayer it's being done in the spirit, and we must believe God, and let him have his way. Now I'm not saying this was the reason why we were separated because he did come to church, but believe me it would have helped our marriage. However, God has a way that is so sweet. Now my husband is serving the Lord, and walking day-by-day giving him all the glory. We are giving God everything and asking him to order our steps and when the devil tries to come in we pray and talk about what we are feeling and we expose that devil quick!

Now was my way of doing things the correct way? Probably not in the eyes of God, but that's what I had to do, because I recognized spirits that was not of God. I did what I thought was best for me at that time. I knew I had to keep focused. No matter what, I had to stay on my knees and always asking God to help me. I did not leave to go live with another man. I did not leave to go back into the world. I left to find me again, and believe it or not I feared God to much, I thought he would never speak to me again, everyday I cried and asked him to forgive me for hurting him. I said to God one day, God I really need to know you still love me, and the peace of God came upon me, oh my God I'll never forget it, his peace fell upon me and from that day I know no matter what, there is nothing we can do to stop God from loving us, nothing.

I had so many people that beat me down with the word of God, there were people that said that's why you are going through changes. But, I knew it was what Olivia had to do. If it was wrong or right, I had to do it. Not knowing it was all for my making, so that God can be glorified in my life. You know during that time God allowed so many sisters to come across my path that was in the same situations I was in or they were on their way down that road. I was even asked the questions, what can I tell another sister? How can I even minister to another, I said I can tell a sister, no matter what you do don't loose focus on God. Ask him to show you the real you. Always, ask God to do it in me first Lord, Clean me up, and when that happens God can and will show up. There were so many scriptures I read, but I lived in **Psalm (91),** I would read the entire psalm, but always focus on verses one and two: "He that dwelleth in the secret place (in prayer) of the most high shall abide under the shadow of the almighty, I will say of the Lord, he is my refuge and my fortress: my God; in him will I trust".

Lets look at the word REFUGE: meaning shelter or protection from danger or distress, a place that provides protection. See my God protected me even when others thought I was wrong or out of order, my God still saw fit to cover me and I praise him every day for his protection. See I needed his protection because I was feeling like I was no longer covered under the blood. The devil would put thoughts in my mind and then there were people who would say things that would make me feel like I was the lowest of the lows, but my God oh how I Love him, he protected me.

Lets look at the word DISTRESS: meaning suffering of body or mind: pain, anguish, trouble, misfortune, a condition of danger or desperate need (to subject to great strain or difficulties, upset). My God, hallelujah glory be to my Father, because sister girl, I was going through, it wasn't easy to walk out and take my child with me, you see him and his daddy were very close. It tore me apart to watch my son cry and hurting, especially at bedtime, when he would say I want my daddy. It was not easy at all. My whole life changed, I cannot stop saying this sister, let go and let God. Your strength lies in the secret place of God. See when you go down distress lane my God, this is what the secret place will do, it will cloth you with fortress, which means: a fortified place (a permanent post). It will strengthen you, give physical strength and endurance, encourages, and enriches you with the vitamins you will need spiritually. Let's turn to **Galatians 5:22**, again, we already had this scripture in the last section, however lets read starting from the 22nd verse," but the fruit of the spirit is love joy, peace, long-suffering, gentleness, goodness, faith, meekness, and temperance". These are the spiritual vitamins we need every day. My God I feel like running, excuse me I have a dance in my feet, hallelujah, hallelujah glory to God, my God my God, sister, sister, sister, if you don't get anything else out of this book, get this "Try God"! Because if he cannot do it, it cannot be done.

To the sister who lost it all, your children, your husband, your job, your self esteem, yes I speak to you my sister, stop feeling like you are filthy rags, stop feeling like you are dirt, let me say something about dirt, see in order for a plant to grow a seed has to be planted in dirt. So my sister I'm planting a seed into your life, the word of God is that seed, and you're the dirt, and Jesus and the spirit of Christ is the water, and light that you need. When we in the natural plant a seed in dirt and water it and give it light we watch it. A few days go by, and something is coming up out of that dirt, and a few days later we see a stem sticking up, and a few day after that we see some buds on the stem, and before we know it we see some colors coming out of those buds, and a week or so we have a beautiful flower. Could it be a peace lily, could it be a myrtle bud, which represent the sweet fragrance of perfume, or could it be a rose, oh my God, the petals of a rose, soft and silky feeling, beautiful just to look at and lace with a silky feeling. So my sister, if you feel like dirt, get ready to bloom because this is your season. To the sister who feels ugly and have an I do not care attitude, let me say this, God created nothing ugly, you are made in the image of God, and you are as beautiful on the inside as you are on the outside. You have a heart that is as big as the world, and you are clothed with grace today, know that woman of God. Stop saying you just don't care about anything anymore. Arise from that place, now! And let the devil know, I serve a God who cares everything about me, how I look, how I feel, and most of how I grow in his love. That's right the more you let God love you the more, you will love.

The more you let God embrace you the more you will embrace others. God called you out of darkness and into his marvelous light. God said take off the garments of heaviness and put on the garment of praise. For victory is yours. Remember this if crying all night long didn't take your mind, if being lower than dirt didn't do it, if being beaten day and night, didn't do it, if being on drugs, didn't do it, if losing your children didn't do it, if being left to die, didn't do it, if being abused didn't do it, then my sister stand up Woman of God, and give God the praise, because if the devil didn't take you out after all this, then he blew his chance, because it's too late now, for you are a new sister. Remember you were created by the Almighty Father, and God created you for a purpose: he created you to live and not die, to be the head and not the tail, to be rich and not poor, to be a blessing and not a curse, to be Saved, Sanctified, and Holy Ghost filled. Get up my sister it is not over, get up! Stay focused, let yourself be teachable by the Holy Ghost, seek God like never before, and make Jesus your very best friend. Remember **Proverbs 18:24** "a man (sister) that hath friends must show himself friendly: and there is a friend that sticketh closer then brother (sister) Jesus". Remember if God cannot do it, it cannot be done. Encourage yourself: Feast on the word of God. **Psalm 27:14** "Wait on the Lord: be of good courage, and he shall strengthen thine heart: wait, I say, on the Lord". What about **Psalm 62:5** "my soul, wait thou only upon God; for my expectation is from him". This is my favorite one **Isaiah 40:31** "they that wait upon the Lord shall renew their strength: they shall mount up with wings as eagles; they shall run, and not be weary, and they shall walk and not faint". I know it's not easy waiting for something to happen, but we must wait on God and his timing. Look at **Habakkuk, 2:3** "for the vision is yet for an appointed time, but at the end it shall speak, and not lie: though it tarry, wait for it; because it will surely come, it will not tarry". Well my sister, I pray these scriptures will penetrate in your hearts.

Here are a few more scriptures to feast on, **Ephesians 4:31–32** "Let all bitterness, and wrath, and anger, and clamor, and evil speaking, be put away from you, with all malice: and be ye kind one to another tenderhearted, forgiving one another, even as God for Christ's sake hath forgiven you." **1Peter 3:1–6** "Like-wise, ye wives, be in subjection to your own husbands; that, if any obey not the word, they also may without the word be won by the conversation of the wives; while they behold your chaste conversation coupled with fear. Whose adorning let it not be that outward adorning of plaiting the hair, and of wearing of gold, or of putting on of apparel; But let it be the hidden man of the heart, in that which is not corruptible, even the ornament of a meek and quiet spirit, which is in the sight of God of great price. For after this manner in the old time the holy women also, who trusted in God, adorned themselves, being in subjection unto their own husband: Even as Sarah obeyed Abraham, calling him lord: whose daughters ye are, as long as ye do well, and are not afraid with any amazement". That scripture I know is a hard pill to swallow, but it is the word of God. Oh we can go on and on in the word of God, because it's the word that changes us. Therefore, I will leave you with some that you can look up. **Joshua 24:15, Psalm 10:2, Proverbs 10:2** and **Proverbs 3:5–6,** let me quote this one," Trust in the Lord with all thine heart and lean not unto thine own understanding. In all thy ways acknowledge him and he shall direct thy path". I end this section with this scripture.

Sisters Of Authority

Sisters of Authority
Sisters in the spot light
Headship
Proverbs 29:2 When the righteous are in authority

I really do not know why God is allowing me to speak or even write this I don't and never had to wear this "hat" lady of authority. However, I feel deep within my spirit, that there is a need for this to be said. I feel that it needs to be a gathering, of all women who are in authority, female Pastors need to find a way to embrace another female Pastor. Whisper, in her ear and tell her a secret that you've been carrying in your heart all your Pastoral years. Let her know that you are not happy at home, your husband doesn't embrace you in his arms, he doesn't tell you he loves you, he doesn't even tell you how pretty you are.

He says nothing at all about nourishing your self esteem. That's right while your are at it tell her you've been walking around with this jealous spirit for years, jealous about how Pastor ladybug always looks good, and her husband showers her with flowers and gifts all the time. Pastor Betty Boo has the finest clothes and it bothers you to see her come into the room. All eyes are always on her. All your life everyone was in the spot light except you. Oh, what is really in the hearts of female Pastors, First Ladies, and big time Female Evangelist? This thing is in my spirit so strong I believe God is saying, for his daughters to find that sister friend and become like little girls growing up, remember your(girlfriend) growing up, your best friend? She use to be able to wear your favorite dress, she would come over and spend the night, sleep in your bed, you would share with her all the time, remember those days? If you had one candy bar, she got half of it. Back then we were so close that we used to drink behind each another. What happened my sisters? A sister needs a sister. A female Pastor needs a female Pastor, if you start telling Pastor Ladybug one secret watch her tell you two, then before you know it Pastor Betty Boo will release some secrets also. Then First lady, will be talking to Sister Evangelist, and hey again, before you know it sisters will be laying down their titles, and releasing deep hidden secrets. Then the enemy is exposed, and we all know once that happens, every chain, is broken, every wall is coming down, and every strong hold loses it grip.

I do not know why but I feel God is saying to the female Pastors it is time to reunite with one another it's time to apologize to one another for not being honest. Apologize for(backbiting), apologize for not supporting one another, and apologize for not praying for one another. Apologize for always trying to out do one another, and most of all apologize for not carrying yourself as a Pastor, First Lady, or even Evangelist should. I encourage you women of authority to take the first step, do what you have to do to start releasing layers of unseen things that is not of God. You come in every day with a smile, and you walk out burdened. You come in looking beautiful and leave out empty, no peace, and no joy, not even laughter. All I can say is I could not end this book, without speaking to my sisters who are in authority. If this penetrates in your soul, then will you take the first step? Call up that sister, the very one you rolled your eyes at just Sunday, that's right call her up. Write that Pastor and support her ministry, after all its for the kingdom of God, hey if she is anointed I am sure she went through, just as you went through. Pray for that sister, fast for her. The next time you see Pastor Betty Boo embrace her and release a secret, and watch and see how many secrets you will have to pray about. My God, sisters when we expose the enemy like this, power from on high will be released. You will become a prayer partner a Sister Touching and Agreeing. Maybe you can start a (P.J.) party, remember those, we would sit up all night and tell stories about what happened at school, or at a party(whatever) it was, conversation was being done. What about a conference just for women of authority, pray about it I believe God will lead you in what to say and how to start a unique conference like that. Call it a Holy Ghost Sleep Over. What ever you do, expose that devil now! Be honest embrace one another and watch the mighty hand of God be upon you. Will you be the first?

Widows

Widows

I speak to the widows, for what ever reason, I had to touch and agree with you my sister as well. Yes, I know God loves us all, but this book would have been incomplete if I did not encourage you my sister. I don't know that place, but I heard a sister speak about how it is when you lose your husband. I do know I serve a Mighty God, I know him by name, El-Shaddai, which means just that all mighty God. Elohim meaning the strong one, El Elon, the most high God, and Elolam the everlasting, God.

I said all that to say this, he is your almighty God; he is the strong one you need in the wee night hours. When you feel weak in your spirit, when you feel like you just can't go any more he is that one you call on Elohim. What about when you feel low? The devil starts throwing thoughts into your mind, things like maybe your husband would still be here if you've only have done this or that. Maybe he's telling you, your last words were the words that killed him, whatever the enemy is trying to do to make you feel lower than dirt, call on El Elyon the most high God, which means, look up to where all your strength comes from. Remember you are never alone ever! Jesus said I would never leave you nor forsake you. Call him by name, Elolam your everlasting God, remember that my sister.

So let the enemy know I must move on with my life and I refuse to let you control me anymore. That's right my sister, get up from that place, stand up tall, that's right, look in the mirror you are looking at a woman of God, strong, bold and blessed, clothed with grace which means you now have favor upon you woman of God. You are now made whole in the Lord. Let the devil know you are renewing your mind with the word of God. Your heart is being made pure day by day, and this temple is the temple of the Holy one Jesus Christ. The word of God tells me where the spirit of the Lord is there is liberty. I am free; I am free, thank God. Hallelujah,

hallelujah. Therefore, my sisters stand up and praise your way into the secret place of God. Lets read Psalm (91). "He that dwelleth in the secret place of the Most High shall abide under the shadow of the Almighty. I will say of the Lord, He is my refuge and my fortress: my God; in him will I trust. Surely, he shall deliver thee from the snare of the fowler, and from the noisome pestilence. He shall cover thee with his feathers, and under his wings shall thou trust: his truth shall be thy shield and buckler. Thou shalt not be afraid for the terror by night; nor for the arrow that flieth by day; nor for the pestilence that walketh in darkness; nor for the destruction that wasteth at noonday". This entire psalm is awesome, however I stopped at verse number six. Read this psalm everyday, it will encourage you, bless you, and cover you with the blood of Jesus. Be prepared to witness to another sister, your testimony will be her strength, trust me, the more you testify about God the more your strength becomes stronger. Your deliverance, your healing, and most of all your elevation in God will take place.

Well sister are your ready to go higher in God? Amen! To God be all the Glory, I want to leave you with some promises of the Lord. If I may, I would like to pray for you, touch, and agree that the will of God will over take your life. Father God in the name of Jesus I do not know this place Oh Lord, but my sister does and I pray that you heal every area of her life that needs that healing touch. Deliver her from every area that she is broken in, every door that the enemy has closed I pray you open them up in Jesus name. I pray oh God that you restore everything that the devil has stolen; create in her oh God a new heart, new desire, and most of all a new love for herself. I know that there is nothing to hard for you.

Well my sister be encourage and watch the hand of God move upon your life. I believe God will place a sister in your life to become your prayer partner. Then you will be able to touch and agree with one another sister, amen. You can write me anytime.

"smile" let me leave you with some scriptures to feast on daily, amen, 1Timothy 5: 3 "Honor widows that are widows in-deed". 1Corinthians 7:8 "I say therefore to the unmarried and widows, it is good for them if they abide even as I. In this scripture, Paul is saying keep yourself for the Lord, stay focus on God". Jeremiah 49:11 "leave thy fatherless children, I will preserve them alive; and let thy widows trust in me". I pray these scripture will keep you in the presence of the Lord.

Help A Sister Out

Well my sister in this society we all need some kind of help, there are all kinds of counseling going on of many kinds, that it has became a part of life. You have children going to counselors or psychologists just to cope in school, the peer pressure is so heavy for them even at the age of (5). You have married couples going to counseling because their marriage is on the verge of breaking up, the lines of communication is down. You have so many people that are on drugs, or have been on drugs for so long that they cannot cope on a day-to-day level, so they need to have counseling to make it. (At least) once a week, they need to sit down and talk to someone to express the stress they are dealing with. In addition, all that is good, but there is nothing better than to talk to someone who can relate.

I say this to say we sisters need a helping hand from another sister, so why not help a sister out. If you find yourself seeing a sister that is younger than you, and her lifestyle is not lady like, and you see her going down the wrong path, why not stop and help a sister out. Let her know what she is doing wrong, and how she can become the real woman that she can be. In this time in age, these young girls just do not have a clue, they are just flowing with the crowd and the crowd is into everything from drugs to a (lifestyle) of lesbians. You have young girls with hearts that will try anything once. Those of you older sisters that have a very strong education, help a sister out. See if you can educate someone, either teach her yourself or walk her in the right direction. What about you sisters who is financially able to fund another sister education, or even place them into their own home, what ever you can do financially why don't you help a sister out. Some of you may say what will I get out of this, well if you seek God and he orders your steps, you'll get his blessing when you least expect it. What about a very strong mother, if you know you have that trait, then maybe you can start up some kind of meeting in your area about helping out young mothers on how to raise up their children.

There are so many ways, we can help a sister out, I'm sure there are thousands of sisters that have a trait in fashion design, you my sister can teach a young girl how to dress, what to put on and what not to wear. What about my beautician's? You can either show a sister how to do her own hair, or you can bless her and have her come to you once every two weeks, what ever you can do to help a sister out, will take you to the next level in life, trust me. There are so many women that don't have physicals on a yearly basis. I have spoken to some that said they have never been to the doctor, my God, what is going on in their bodies. Some say they just do not have the money. If we women gynecologist would just do at least (5) free visits or even something of a low-income type of thing, I am sure that would be helping a sister. If you are a sister and have your own business, you can do something for a sister. Maybe you are a sister who has a home and no one lives there but you. I'm sure there's a sister that is in need of a place? If so open your home, just to help a sister out, she don't have to stay there forever, hey give her a time period, and after that she's on her own. I see so many women suffering in so many areas; they just need someone to redirect them in the right path.

Low self-esteem over takes us and before you know it there is no life at all. I thank God for my mother; you talking about a strong woman, oh my God, she would always say become your own woman. She never once taught me anything about racism; we were brought up to respect our elders, no matter the skin color. In her own way she taught us to appreciate the rainbow of skin colors that God created, I have to mention this because there is so must prejudice going around, that it stops the very flow of life. When it comes to disagreements choose your battles very carefully. Don't close the doors of communications to little things, like leg-shaving, clothing tastes, or hair styles. Hey if a sister wants to try or do something new let her, if it's not life threatening, let her try it at least once. Praise and reward a sister, no matter how small, even if it is just her manners, tell her. Make sure you're happy and secure, because only a strong sister can cultivate a strong sister. Maybe you don't have a daughter or you don't even know of a sister that may need help. If that be the case, hey there are so many young girls who need a mother figure in their lives, check with churches, or go through the school system, maybe you can check into some type of halfway home for women, what ever the case maybe, do get involved.

I would like to just encourage a sister to help a sister out, if I can pray a prayer it would be, Father God in the name of Jesus, I pray that you will order my sister steps, teach her how to interact with another sister, allow her to release her strength, her love and her hope into another sister. Maybe she herself needs to be delivered from some things, I pray that walls are knocked down, I pray that doors are being open, and any doors that need to be closed, I pray oh God that you close them. However, oh God you see fit to use your daughters I pray you order our steps, don't let us miss an opportunity to bless some young girl, to teach them how to become a strong woman. Don't let us get so set in our ways that nothing else matters. I pray for those that you have blessed to become professional, I pray that they have compassion and will minister in a way of giving. Teach us my father in Jesus name I pray. Well my sister I end this section with this prayer and I do pray some way and some how we do help a sister out.

Mothers and Daughters

Mothers and Daughters

Many women feel guilty about things they have no control over. Have you ever noticed how hard it is to communicate? Through out my life I can remember stories way back when I was a young girl, my friends would tell me stories about their relationship with their mothers. My one friend would also say her mother never had time for her or the family, either the job came first, or the other child came before her. She never could talk with her mother. She is now 37 years old and that scar has been with her all these years. Could it be that her mother had no control over that? Maybe it was how her mother was brought up, maybe her mother's, mother would not allow her to express her feelings, so that's what was installed in her. She did not know how to communicate. All she knew was she was not allowed to express her feelings. If you are in such a place, then we need to touch and agree that this stronghold becomes broken.

Communication is something that we need to do no matter what, when you communicate you express your opinion, you send a message verbally. A mother should be able to communicate with her daughter, for more reasons than one. There will come a time in your daughter's life that she will need to know the history of her family, the family line, and if she does not know then she is incomplete without being rooted in her family lifeline. There will come a time that your daughter will need to know the truth about life and how life begins. What about just open conversation, what if your daughter just wants to be close with her mother, it is up to you mothers, to make sure you keep the lines of communication open with your daughter. There are going to be times that your daughter may need you to tell her about growing years, staying healthy, which will help her understand, and prevent health problems. What about emotional needs and sexual concerns? Your daughter needs you to open up to her. I pray that God will open up this door. Moms do not blame yourself for things that you had no control over. Your past is over and today is a new day, so ask God to help you overcome this stronghold, and to order steps from this day forward. I believe God will show you all you need to know about opening up to release all that's within you.

Daughters, daughters its now up to you that you don't allow that strong hold to roll over into your life, you must be able to look, listen and obey and start with a new look on life. I have a friend who says that she just cannot talk to her daughter, it is either yelling to the top of their lungs, or there is silence. Her daughter is eighteen years of age. Could it be that this is a generation curse? What ever it may be we need to be able to talk to one another. Let's pray about every door the enemy tries to come in. Father God in the name of Jesus, I pray oh God that you bless your mothers, teach them how oh God to minister to their daughters. Open up the lines of communication father God that they may be able to express themselves freely. Allow them to become friends, while the respect of motherhood is still in tact. I do not really know the percentage of a Mother/Daughter relationships as far as a disconnection, but I do know that there is a problem with mothers and daughters. There are mothers in the world today that will date their daughter's boyfriend, even will have an affair with their husband. Something is wrong, and if that has happened to you and you are the Mother you need to first ask God to forgive you and then ask your daughter to forgive you also. Then you both need to seek the face of God to help you get through this. Something like this is a hard pill to swallow, but our heavenly father can and will restore.

If you are a daughter that is hurting, I pray God will strengthen you, will give you the peace that you need to endure, and I pray that you don't let anything come between you and your mother, you only have one and I don't care what she did, ask God to help you with whatever you are going through. It may be a daughter dating mom's boyfriend, whatever it may be, "sisters you must reconnect". To hear something like this just blows my mind. I will never ever understand why something like this happens. I will say this, women we got some stuff with us! If we don't watch it the devil will take completely over our lives, jealously will creep in, you'll become jealous of your own mother or sister, why? Nevertheless, it happens. That is because we feel like it is all about us, and it is not! There is and will always be another woman that look's better, dress better, and carry her self better than we do.

We need to be able to encourage each other, especially moms, encourage your daughter, she's a part of you, hey if she's got it going on, be proud of your seed, because after all she's a product of you.

I thank God for my mother, I don't hang out with her every day like my sister does, because they do things that I don't do, did the devil try to mess with my mind? Yes, all the time, but see the difference is my mother impacted me with her love I have no doubt that my mother doesn't love me, no doubt at all, and as far as my sister, never has she tried to rub it in, that her and mommy spend more time together then we do. I thank God cause my family is very close and no matter what we are there for each other. I just want to encourage a mother or a daughter, let God work it out. Trust me if you give it to him, my Lord, he will turn it all around and get the glory. Trust him. For whatever reason, I pray this section of the book encourages you, and remember put God first and spend time in the bible and seeking God in prayer. Here are some scriptures that will strengthen you.

Psalm 9:10 "and they that know thy name will put their trust in thee: for thou, Lord, hast not forsaken them that seek thee".

Psalm 27:10 "when my father and my mother forsake me, then the Lord will take me up"

1Peter 5:7 "casting all your care upon him; for he careth for you".

Isaiah 49:15 "can a woman forget her sucking child, that she should not have compassion on the son of her womb? Yea, they may forget, yet will I not forget thee?"

Ephesians 4:31 "let all bitterness, and wrath, and anger, and clamour, and evil speaking, be put away from you, with all malice: and be ye kind one to another, tenderhearted, forgiving one another, even as God for Christ's sake hath forgiven you". I pray these scripture will strengthen you and your family. Like I said in the last section, mothers keep the lines of communication open, remember, your opinion is just that, your opinion. Your daughter has her own opinion also. "Don't sweat the small stuff."

How To Raise Our Children

How do we really raise our children? Well with me, it was all hands on experience. My mother has and still is teaching me, and I am 45 years old. I remember when I had my oldest son, he was like a baby doll to me, until I wanted to go out and party on the weekends, and I realized I could not leave him home like I would a doll baby. You talk about responsibility, it hit me hard, I was a mother and I had to respond as a mother should and would. I was not a woman that was brought up in church or even knew how to raise up a child in a Christian life style. I speak for the single mother because there was a time in my life that I was single and it was hard at times to raise my son. I had to work and keep up with the everyday things because he wanted the latest in clothing and plus he always wanted to stay focused on what was going on. Not one time did I speak badly about his father. I guess I was blessed because he was able to see his father everyday if he wanted to.

However, his father was not the father that he should have been in my son's life. I never spoke any negative words about his father at all. But all those years my son was watching and observing, and to this day everything he saw he is speaking now. The life style that my son chose to live, made me feel I was a failure in motherhood, and for a period of time that's what I dealt with, but one day the grace of God let me know, you did all you could do, and your son made his own choices. He is dealing with the ups and downs of life. However, I know God can and will keep my son. I remember when my son was about sixteen years old, I tried to get him involved in church but he made the choice of living in the street, dealing with drugs and other street living. I was not able to bring him up in the way of the Lord. If I could encourage you single mothers, raise your children in the way he should go when they become grown. Proverbs 22:6 says" train up a child in the way he should go and when he is old, he will not depart from it".

This means that what we instill in our children it will not leave them. If we bring them up to respect their elders, no matter how old they are, they will always have respect for people older than them. If we teach them responsibility at an early age, then when they become an adult, they will be able to handle the ups and downs of life. Oh, how I wish that I had raised my son in the fear of the Lord. Whether, he would be in jail or not I really cannot say, but if he was brought up under the law of the Lord, he would have thought twice before doing wrong. For the mothers who have sons and daughters, that are not living the life they should be, I want to encourage you, God has and still is keeping my son, it's never to late, I believe my son listens when I pray and when I tell him to put and keep God first. I will end this section with we as parents must some way, and some how, train up our children in the fear of the Lord, and then trust them with the Lord. .

Your Body Is The Temple Of God

YOUR BODY IS THE TEMPLE OF GOD
Roman 12:1 says "I beseech (beg) you by the mercies of God, that ye present your bodies a living sacrifice, holy, acceptable unto God".

Whether we are walking with the Lord or not we are the creation of God. When we were created, he created us into his own image, we were to look like him, act like him, and carry ourselves like him. This body is to house the spirit of Christ. Therefore, we must live a healthy life. I just want to mention a few tips on how to live a healthy life, I am sure we have read and heard a million times about living right and healthy and how to do it. If I could just give some simple pointers just to get you started, for myself I struggle with this everyday, but everyday I try.

First, let me release some good eating habits. First let us look at the food pyramid. At the top of the pyramid it is divided into two, you must have **2–3 servings** out of this group, which is your **(milk, yogurt, and Cheese Group.)** The other half of this portion you should also have **2–3 servings** of, **(meats Poultry, Fish, Dry Beans, Eggs, and Nuts).** The middle section of this pyramid is divided into two parts, which is your Vegetables and Fruits; you should have **3–5 servings of Vegetable** and **2–4 servings of your fruits**. The bottom portion is your Breads, Cereal, Rice and Pasta; you should have 6–11 servings of these each day. Now how to use this daily Food Guide: what counts as a serving. Your bread group **(1 slice of bread, ½ cup of cooked rice or pasta, ½ cup of cooked cereal and 1 ounce of ready to eat cereal.).** Your milk group, **(1 cup of milk or yogurt and ½ to 1 ounce of cheese).** Vegetables **(½ cup of chopped raw or cooked vegetables and 1 cup of leafy raw vegetables).** Fruits **(1 piece of fruit or melon wedge).** Your Meat, Poultry, Fish, Dry Beans Eggs and nuts **(2–1/2 to 3 ounce of cooked lean meat, poultry or fish, Count ½ cup of cooked beans, or 1 egg, or 2 tablespoons of peanut butter as 1 ounce of lean meat)** this will count as about 1/3 serving. This very small tip of the pyramid, shows the Fats, oils, and sweets. These are foods such as salad dressing, cream. butter, margarine, sugars, soft drinks, candies and sweet desserts. These foods provide calories, and very few vitamins and minerals. Most people should go easy on foods from this group.

Now let's do a little exercise, the safest way to me is walking, do what you can but you should do at least 30 minutes a day. You can do 15 in the morning, and 15 in the evening, but you should get 30 minutes at least 4 times a week. Now the correct way of walking, I have read repeatedly, to walk with your chin up, shoulders relaxed and chest lifted. Pump arms with a 90-degree with elbows. Your hands should be cupped loosely, not clenched. Pull abs in; keep knees soft, plant heel first with toes lifted, then roll foot along ground pushing off with the toes. Maintain a tall posture do not arch your back or lean forward. Remember, my sister this is only from my experience, and if we stick to this, we will not only lose weight, but we will also be able to stay healthy. Really, that is the most important thing, that we stay healthy.

We cannot forget our water, we must drink at least 8–8 ounces of water a day, do not forget **DRINK THE WATER**. For the sister who is really having a hard time in this area pray and ask God to help you, he'll either send someone your way and he'll strengthen your determination and before you know it girlfriend you'll be up and looking good. I remember I went from a size 11–12 to a size 22 and girl you talk about low self-esteem, I had it and it brought me down. But one day I prayed and my life changed, I changed my eating habits and started walking, I'm now in a size 14 and if I don't stick to it that weight will over take me again. You can do it and it can be done. Be proud of who you are and work on being a better person. No matter what, we first must love ourselves.

You know I do not know how true this is but I have read that the pearl is symbolism of health. Oh, how we can become the pearl of beauty, let me mention this about a pearl, they have always decorated crowns and robes, Kings and Queens wear them, so my sister think of yourself as the Queen, and wear your crown. Pearls come in a wide variety of sizes, shapes and colors. In addition, they are very attractive. Did you know they are formed in the sea? Well they are, in every oyster there lies the ability to produce a pearl. I just thought you may wanted to know that. Then this way you'll want to become the woman God created you to be. There is a purpose for you my sister, and we must position ourselves to be ready. Hey, you never know you may be the one to encourage another sister to lose weight, to stay healthy, and to be proud of herself. If God can use anybody, he can use you. Take one day at a time, and do one thing at a time. Sit down, write you out a planner, and go by that, make one for 7 days and follow it every day, and while you are at it, get a journal, and keep it, and watch the hand of God move in your life. You can do it my sister I know you can. Start your day off with prayer, eat right, do your exercises, clear your mind, and hold your head up and say Lord I commit my day to you, and when your day is over make sure you end it with prayer. Well my sister, I will end this section and hope that it is food for your very soul, and remember your are the king's daughter, ACT LIKE IT!

Walking In Your Ministry

What can I say, after all we have been through. All the hallways, alleys ways, by ways and highways; we must walk on the road of our calling. How do we get there, first we must give ourselves to the Lord, we must dedicate our lives to Christ, and then some way and some how, he'll minister to us and doors will open up, and some doors will close, but however, he sees fit to change our lives, it will put us on the right path.

I am reminded when I heard the voice of God. First, it was when my mother was having heart surgery, which is when I turned my life over to the Lord. From the beginning of that call, God would have people come into my life and would teach me all that I needed to learn at that time in my life. I went through a period of just going to church, watching and looking, listening and watching. I did not know anything else but to go to church, and read my bible. I did not know who was who, and what that person had to do, the only person that I knew was the Pastor. However, as time went on I found out that the Pastor and ministers ran the church. I started really reading my bible and I would pray Lord teach me all that I need to know, and that's what happened, the Holy Ghost would show me day by day how to pray, what to pray for and when to pray. One day I was in my salon doing hair and a couple of the ladies were talking about a service that was happening that weekend, and they went on and on, and one of them mentioned the name Evangelist Moses. Now I had heard that name so many times, and I would get excited like I knew her and really I never laid eyes on this woman. As time went on I found myself going to one of her services.

I went to a women's conference that she was speaking at, and it was at that service, that I felt fire in my stomach, I mean, as if a match was struck in the very pit of my stomach. I really did not understand it, but I knew it was God. I said that to say, if we are seeking we'll find him. From that service on, this woman took me up under her wings and taught me everything that I needed to know at that time in my early walk with the Lord. This woman was a woman of prayer. We would pray all the time. There were time we would pray every day, if we did not meet at her house we all met on the phone. I remember she was speaking at this church out of town, and when we got there we only saw (3) people, and I was looking for a crowd. However, you know I learn that God moves on those that are in need. That service was so awesome, it was as if the church was packed. That was an experience. God knew it would stir up my spirit man. All that praying, positioned me to except services like that. The bible says prayer and fasting will release great power. Oh how she would fast, she would always say," baby turn your plate down". (Give up a meal) and seek the face of God". "She was laying a foundation in my life, and making sure it was a solid foundation. Once she trained me in that way, she started teaching me in the word of God. We would have bible study, and we would always go to the bible, that is what I really love about her, she never gave her opinion she would say let's find it in the word. This woman has impacted my life with great holiness. When we would have services she would use me at times to introduce her, or expedite the service, but in her own way she would pull out the ministry that was in us. She would always say" baby it is in you, and you do not belong to me you belong to God". In addition, I would just watch her life, because I learn how to live holy, I learn how to seek the face of God. I learn how to be still in the present of the Lord. She would say guard your spirit; do not let just anything get into your spirit. In addition, I was like a sponge soaking up everything that my spirit man was receiving.

There were so many people in and out of my life when it came to my walk with the Lord. I must praise God for my Pastor and his wife, Bishop Richard and first Lady Debbie Williford. The teaching that was instilled in me under my pastor, was the meat of the word of God. He spoke the infallible word of God. That speaks for it self. I just felt led to release this info, maybe for a sister that does not know if she has been called. We have all been called, we are all ministers either in the pulpit or in the street. Let me say this, seek the face of God and the Holy Ghost will order your steps. The bible tells us in **Second Timothy 2:15** "Study to show thyself approved unto God, a workman that needeth not to be ashamed, rightly dividing the word of truth". Therefore, if we search the scriptures and seek the face of God, we will learn all we need to know as we walk down the road of ministry. So, if I can encourage you my sister, position yourself to be use by God at any given time. Know the word, and keep a prayer ready, ask God to help you to witness to the lost. Oh, how the time is right to be used by God. This is the hour the harvest is ripe, and you are the one that will be hand picked. Sister girl, be that woman of godly living. We all have been called to go higher in God. He called us to live a godly life, we must let our light shine, we need to know how to live Holy, and living Holy is staying at the feet of Jesus. See if we stay there, He'll teach us how to dress, how to carry ourselves and how to use words of grace and wisdom. What about discipline? We are to be able to discipline ourselves to the point of controlling our emotions, our behavior and how we react in a situation that needs to be in control.

We should always have words of encouragement for people that come across our path. Wives we must be able to minister to our husbands. Single sisters don't be impatient you'll never know what married women, God will have come across your path. This women will be able to minister to you, she'll be able to show you through the word of God and also through her own experiences. We must also be able to minister to our families; we have to know how to divide our time with our children. Let us look at **Proverbs 31**, starting at the tenth verse," who can find a virtuous woman? For her price is far above rubies. The heart of her husband doth safely trust in her, so that he shall have no need of spoil. She will do him good and not evil all the days of her life. She seeketh wool, and flax, and worketh willingly with her hands. She is like the merchants ships' she bringeth her food from afar. She riseth also while it is yet night, and giveth meat to her household, and a portion to her maidens. She considereth a field, and buyeth it: with the fruit of her hands she planteth a vineyard. She girdeth her loins with strength, and strengtheneth her arms. She perceiveth that her merchandise is good: her candle goeth not out by the night. She layeth her hands to the spindle, and her hands hold the distaff. She stretcheth out her hand to the poor; yea, she reacheth forth her hands to the needy. She is not afraid of the snow for her household: for all her household are clothed with scarlet". Oh what a woman! Oh what a woman! You see when God calls us to a place, he'll order ours steps, there is no way we in our own strength, can walk like a virtuous woman. However, through the grace of our heavenly Father we can do all things. So my sister meditate on this word day and night, let it penetrate in your very heart and some way and some how the Holy Spirit will show you how to become a woman that's been called by God. I end this with, let God have his way in your life.

Nuggets

✤

Jesus is your...

Saviour: **Titus 3:5,6** "Not by works of righteousness which we have done, but according to his mercy he saved us, by the washing of regeneration, and renewing of the Holy Ghost; which he shed on us abundantly through Jesus Christ our Saviour;"

Luke 19:10 "For the son of man is come to seek and to save that which was lost".

John 3:16 "For God so loved the world, that he gave his only begotten Son, that whosoever believeth in him should not perish, but have everlasting life".

Roman 3:24,25 "Being justified freely by his grace through the redemption that is in Christ Jesus: whom God hath set forth to be a propitiation through faith in his blood, to declare his righteousness for the remission of sins that are past, through the forbearance of God".

Ephesians 2:4,5 "But God, who is rich in mercy, for his great love wherewith he loved us, Even when we were dead in sins, hath quickened us together with Christ, (by grace ye are saved;)"

John 6:47 "Verily, Verily, I say unto you, He that believeth on me hath everlasting life".

Ephesians, 2:8,9 "For by grace are ye saved through faith; and that not of yourselves: it is the gift of God: Not of works, lest any man should boast".

Romans 10:9 "That if thou shalt confess with thy mouth the Lord Jesus and shalt believe in thine heart that God hath raised him form the dead, thou shalt be saved".

He's our everything

Philippians 4:13 "I can do all things through Christ which strengtheneth me".

Romans 8:37 "Nay, in all these things we are more than conquerors through him that loved us".

Philippians 4:19 "But my God shall supply all your need according to his riches in glory by Christ Jesus.

1John 3:22 And whatsoever we ask, we receive of him, because we keep his commandments, and do those things that are pleasing in his sight".

Mark 11:24 "Therefore I say unto you, what things soever ye desire, when ye pray, believe that ye receive them, and ye shall have them".

2Corinthians 5:17 "Therefore if any man be in Christ, he is a new creature: old things are passed away; behold, all things are become new".

John 15:7 "If ye abide in me, and my words abide in you, ye shall ask what ye will, and it shall be done unto you".

The word of God has no error

2Timothy 3:16 "All scripture is given by inspiration of God, and is profitable for doctrine, for reproof, for correction, for instruction in righteousness".

Hebrews 4:12 "For the word of God is quick, and powerful, and sharper than any two-edged sword, piercing even to the dividing asunder of soul and spirit, and of the joints and marrow, and is a discerner of the thoughts and intents of the heart".

1Peter 1:23 "Being born again, not of corruptible seed, but of incorruptible, by the word of God, which liveth and abideth for ever".

Psalm 33:9 "For he spake, and it was done; he commanded, and it stood fast.

Psalm 119:89 For ever, O Lord, thy word is settled in heaven".

Psalm 33:6 "By the word of the Lord were the heavens made; and all the host of them by the breath of his mouth".

Isaiah 55:10,11 "For as the rain cometh down, and the snow from heaven, and returneth not thither, but watereth the earth, and maketh it bring forth and bud, that it may give seed to the sower, and bread to the eater: So shall my word be that goeth forth out of my mouth: it shall not return unto me void, but it shall accomplish that which I please, and it shall prosper in the thing whereto I sent it".

How to grow spiritually

2Peter 3:18 "But grow in grace, and in the knowledge of our Lord and Saviour Jesus Christ. To him be glory both now and for ever. A-men".

1Timothy 4:15 "Meditate upon these things; give thyself wholly to them; that thy profiting may appear to all".

1Peter 2:2,3 "As newborn babes, desire the sincere milk of the word, that ye may grow thereby: If so be ye have tasted that the Lord is gracious".

2Peter 1:5–8 "And beside this, giving all diligence, add to your faith virtue; and to virtue knowledge; and to knowledge temperance; and to temperance patience; and to patience godliness; and to godliness brotherly kindness; and to brotherly kindness charity. For if these things be in you, and abound, they make you that ye shall neither be barren no unfruitful in the knowledge of our Lord Jesus Christ".

Ephesians 3:14–19 "For this cause I bow my knees unto the Father of our Lord Jesus Christ, of whom the whole family in heaven and earth is named, that he would grant you, according to the riches of his glory, to be strengthened with might by his spirit in the inner man; that Christ may dwell in your hearts by faith; that ye, being rooted and grounded in love, May be able to comprehend with all saints what is the breadth, and length, and depth, and height; and to know the love of Christ, which passeth knowledge, that ye might be filled with all the fullness of God".

Colossians 1:9–11 "For this cause we also, since the day we heard it, do not cease to pray for you, and to desire that ye might be filled with the knowledge of his will in all wisdom and spiritual understanding; that ye might walk worthy of the Lord unto all pleasing, being fruitful in every good work, and increasing in the knowledge of God; strengthened with all might, according to his glorious power, unto all patience and long-suffering with joyfulness".

Colossians 3:16 "Let the word of Christ dwell in you richly in all wisdom; teaching an admonishing one another in psalms and hymns and spiritual songs, singing with grace in your hearts to the Lord".

Psalm 92:12 "the righteous shall flourish like the palm tree: he shall grow like a cedar in Lebanon".

Singles

I feel I need to start off with scripture, there are so many single sisters in the world today that either don't know the word of God, read it and don't understand it, or just don't care what the word says. Let us look at **1Corinthians 7:32–34** But I would have you without carefulness. He that is unmarried careth for the things that belong to the Lord, how he may; please the Lord: but he that is married careth for the things that are of the world, how he may please his wife (husband). There is a difference also between a wife and a virgin. The unmarried woman careth for the things of the Lord, that she may be holy both in body and in spirit: but she that is married careth for the things of the world, how she may please her husband. Single sisters have the upper hand on married sisters. See when God calls me to pray I have to get up early like 3:30 or so to spend that still time with him, because if not my husband will be up and my son will be getting up, so I have to steal my time from my family to spend with God in the wee morning hours. With you, my single sister and no children, you can spend hours upon hours with the Lord, when he calls you to prayer, that is the advantage singles, have. You can worship the Lord whenever and however you please. You can lay prostrate on the floor in your house and worship and no one will annoy you. That is very important if you are single.

Often we hear unmarried women complain about wanting a husband. Are you complaining about how you need someone? My sister, take advantage of this single life, "girl" you can be sold out! for God, you don't have to cook every night, wash clothes and most of all clean up behind other's. Girl stop praying for a husband and pray that God will anoint you to take care of him. What I mean by that is you must minister to Gods needs. You must first be faithful to the Lord and then he will be faithful to you. If you cannot find it in God, then you will miss it in a man. You must be able to say Lord, I am so glad I have you in my life, you are the one who keeps me going. You are the lover of my soul, my mind, my emotions, my attitude and my every thing. If you oh God embrace me then I will be, strengthen.

Single and loving it, yes you should every second that you have to be with the Lord. You should be able to represent patience like never before. What about your virginity? This is the most precious thing that a woman has, and if you still have the key to your virginity praise God my sister, keep doing what ever you are to keep you covered. There are so many single women that has lost their virginity, and don't know what to do. They feel like that are not worthy or they will never be what God called them to be. Let me say this God has and will forgive you. Just remember you can start your life over before the Lord, repent and let God keep you and raise you up to be the woman he called you to be. Being single does not mean, living for the weekend, it does not mean that you can dress as a street woman, exposing your body. It does not mean that you can date every Joe Blow and sell yourself short. It does not mean that you can say I am young single free and loving it. You just may be the one God uses to stay a virgin. Stay holy, stay at the feet of Jesus until your Boaz (Mr. Right) comes," you just may be the one". So sister girl, stay at the feet of Jesus. Maybe you're the one who lost your virginity, if so just be ready, because God is remaking you, from the inside out, he's taking away thoughts, memories, and shame, just to place you where you need to be at this time in your life. Being single, how do your day start? Can you honestly answer that? Does it start with meeting Jesus early in the morning? If so then how much time do you spend with him before you enter into the world? Could it be just a minute, five minutes, or hours? Being single, your prayer life should be hours upon hours with the Lord. When that happens you will be able to say Lord, I am not so busy that I do not have time for you. It's in you oh God that I move, live and have my being. You'll be able to say Lord, let me be teachable I'll be able to listen to the women of wisdom, women of faith, and women of confidence. I really do not know what it is like to be single and living for the Lord, because when I turned my life over to the lord I was married. A woman that messed up big time in so many areas in my life. The only thing I can remember when I was living as a single person was running the street and living for the weekend, and as I look back, I was waking up with a hangover from drinking and drugging. Losing my body to a man, that did not deserve me at all. But at that time in my life I didn't know no better, but God has kept me over the years, and I truly do thank him, cause it could have been worse than what it was, plus there were friends that didn't make it as far as I did. During those single years, I lost my virginity; I lost trust in a man, which made me to build walls, which kept me living within those walls. Peace was something I never had, because I was always running from one relationship to another. I say all this to say, sister thank God for your singleness, ask him to keep you under the shadow of his protection.

I'm sure there are sister that are single and not by choice, maybe your husband left you, maybe you're a widow, whatever the reason, trust God, I believe, God will not allow you to suffer and he sit back and not step in. Yes, you may be a mother that has children and it is very, very hard, but know that he will be the father to the fatherless, and a judge of the widows. I dare you to trust God totally, and watch him move. Pray as if you've never prayed before, follow his steps in every area of your life. In order for you to truly see the hand of God upon your life, you must put him first, you must! Those days of no food on the table, will turn into groceries for a month, out of no where! God will send someone with food for a month if needed. Your babies needing shoes, will turn into owning more then one pair of shoes. He will take you out of that too small of a living quarters and put you into your own home. If you are sold out to him, by living the life as a righteous saint, trust me God has to move, he says I put my name above my word, so if you call on the name of Jesus, he has to show up.

A Sister Testimony

I realize even at ages 4 to 5 years old God was with me. My mother was an alcoholic, my father walked out on us at an early age. I can remember a police officer being called to my mother's home. She in turn was out cold. He made a statement if neither of us had any knowledge of our next of kin. We would be placed in a foster home. My little sister and older brother would be placed in separate foster homes. That meant siblings that I grew up together with and shared hunger pains together cried together would be separated. Can you imagine at my age being taken away from my family. I would watch my older brother take water from the faucet and put it in a baby bottle and give it to my 2-year sister. He did not have milk to give her. My mother was so drunk he really did not know what else to do.

After being taken to my aunt that night. She contacted my father. He took us south to North Carolina to be with our great grandmother. My mother had no idea that her children were being taking away from her. I never laid eyes on her until I turned 18 years of age and pregnant with my daughter.

The memories of my mother are not what you would consider as the happy family with the white picket fence. However, at 18 years of age I joined her in Connecticut. I finally needed my mother. I was excited and angry. However, I needed her help with raising a child. I had no knowledge of taking care of a newborn. When I moved in with her, she acted like the typical mom. One day I came home from work and there she was drinking. It is funny how at that time I had no knowledge of ever living with her. Nor did I remember her drinking at an early age. How could any mother allow her children to go through the turmoil that we had endured, physically and mentally?

When I finally got married, I would ask my husband to keep the light on. I felt that men just could do what they wanted and nothing would or could be said to stop them. I tried to explain about my abuse as a young girl growing up, but he had the attitude of unconcern, it was like get over it. My uncles and cousins molested and sexual abused me as a little girl. I believe one time I actually hated men. Now, when I hear about abuse to women it upsets me, the spirit upsets me. How can you hurt or abuse someone. The only one who understood what I was going through was my Lord and savior Jesus Christ.

Here I am now in a loveless marriage looking for a way out. I met someone that I had true feelings, or thought I did at that time. I knew this person for 20 years. Therefore, you can see many demonic spirits that possess my mom had tried to take a toll on me. I was finally able to let this useless relationship go. The years alone just toying with past relationships and clinging to men in general was some of the characteristics of my Mother. For years, it kept me in misery. Finally, I was able to let go and let God. It is amazing how much bondage we can allow ourselves to get in. When we are not living according to God's will. If I had been in his word and seeking him daily I would have known only true love comes from him. No man can fill that void. It finally got to the point I could not deal with the pain and tears in my heart. I had to let go and I thought oh, God what do I do now. I kept coming back to this person thinking oh, this is my soul mate. Not knowing his heart was not of God. He did not have a clue as how to treat a woman of God. He finally moved out of the state and I was saying oh God, what now. I cannot just jump up and leave my job.

I believe God allowed this situation in my life just to bring me back to his closeness. About 4 years ago, there was a time that it was just God and I but I allowed a man to come between us and I put God on the back burner if I may say it like that.

The last time we broke up I felt the hand of God restoring me, but this time I understood some of the drama I went through, it was all for the restoration of God giving me a heart like his. I had to learn how to love this man again. In a godly way or as God had chosen to love me. I forgave him in my heart and found that my greatest Love is and will always be my wonderful Father from above. Who loved me unconditionally from the time of my birth? I should have been holding onto the true words from God.

I realize now that my mother is no longer with me. Since that, time I found and know of one that will never leave nor forsake me. He was and is now closer than my only mother. I say it because, I have experienced him (Jesus) as my Lord, Mother, my friend and now my husband. All of those lonely days and nights I spent laying in bed in my room at my great grandmother's home and felling alone and insecure he was right there with me. It is so great to know I was not alone then and I am not alone now. There is no natural man or woman on this earth that could ever fulfill the voids in my life that Jesus has.

Now that I am older with a grown daughter, and a grandson and have been down the pathway of uncertainties I can now trust and lean on the solid rock (Jesus). I now understand things or some of the things my mother went through. My heart goes out to her, because she obviously did not trust Jesus enough. She gave up on life, leaving her children, grandchildren, and now great grandson. She never really has known them or me.

That curse of low self-esteem, the devil tried his best to put me into bondage with it. When God's word says his purpose is to "rob, steal and kill". Watch out, that's his purpose, and he will never steers from his purpose.

I sometimes imagine what my mother's life would have been like had she desired to hold onto God's unchanging hand. I can say she would have lived a fulfilled life. Full of love and happiness had she chose life in lieu of death. Life's toll and the death of my father gave her no incentive to go on living.

The devil had me marked for the same destruction as my mother. What the devil meant for bad God turned it into something good. I thank God somehow, he kept me rooted and grounded in his word and with strong Christian people. For me to say I never thought of taking my life, or felt that I was so in love with someone. I just could not live without them I would be lying. It was a struggle, but God gave me something and someone to hold onto during the molding period of my life.

I did not have a clue and I didn't know then how much Jesus loves me, he knew from my birth, I was a fighter, and that I was worth his loving spirit lingering in me, and one-day I would feel it and become the vibrant, virtuous women he is molding in me.

I never really had the chance to tell her I loved her. We spent so much time arguing and disagreeing on so many life's issues. I regret she died without me saying Mom, I love you, and I understand why you handled this the way you did. You did not realize just how much you could have had all the riches in heaven and peace of mind through Christ Jesus. Mom if you only had walked in Faith and not by Sight. I would tell her I forgive you for leaving me and not having the strength, you should have had. I would say I have felt your pain and my heart hurts that the enemy played such a big part in your death or you wanting to die. God is the only one with that authority. I believe God heard your cry I know he did. That is why he sent our great grandmother in our lives to raise us and bring us up in a Christian home. You just happen to be a weak vessel but know that he has strengthen your daughters are standing strong and encouraging the ones that are not. The enemy may have caused great harm to you but your daughter has become a strong warrior of the Lord.

I believe now she would be very proud of me. I have not allowed my circumstances to take advantage of situations that may arise. I have worked hard and raised my daughter with much respect. I learned I could do all things through Christ who strengthen me. I remember my Mother as a child watching her go through periods of abuse. I was a little girl I did not know how to say, mom pray your way out of the situations you are being attacked.

Now that I am older, I realize man had a lot to do with my mother not holding on to life itself. She gave up totally after my father died. She in turn died afterwards. That is something, to have that kind of love for a man and not God. I knew that generation curse had to be broken. Now I know as below why my spirit man would always say to me trust no man, he knew that if I had not found him when I did, the same things that happened to my mother may have happened ed to me. Now I pray and talk to my daughter about keeping God first. I watched my mother give her precious life up for my father and he continually living his worldly living. He never came to her rescue or console or maybe explains why he left her with three children to take care of by herself. I thank God after all of this I did learn to love them both.

Thank God even at the age of four my spirit was geared into his spirit. I sometimes think about my mother and her life now at the age of 48. What she must have been feeling and going through to have your children taken away from you. To wake up for weeks and not know where your children are. I am sure my dad took his own time telling her we were in another state. My family wanted nothing to do with her. She was so alone. She died alone. Never having her heart filled with joy and love. To all who care to know? If we seek the kingdom of God. A lot of heartaches can and will be avoided. Let us teach our children this as they teach their children. The hold the enemy thought he had on my family. Through the help of God it has broken. I intend to pass it down from generations to generations as long as God allows me. So my sister I pray this testimony encourages somebody.

Every sister goes through something, and if we do not tell it we cannot be deliver nor will we be able to help another sister out. Remember you are not the only one going through. There is a sister out there somewhere that went through what you either did or is going through now. I just pray that you are ready to pray a sister through when a sister stands in need of a prayer.

About the Author

A woman of God that has been hand picked and chosen for such a time as this.

Olivia Thames, born in Norristown Pa, a town outside of Philadelphia, An ordinary girl living in the city, day by day being molded and shaped into God's image. Forty-four years later, residing in North Carolina saved, Holy Ghost filled and still being molded and shaped for the glory of God. Down through the years some awesome Pastors, Evangelists, Prophets and saints of God fed her. Her walk with the Lord is going on ten years, and she continues to stay on the straight and narrow in order to enter through those pearly gates. Her desire is to make heaven her home.

From the Author: Sister girl, remember we are Touching and Agreeing. (Matthew 18:20)
E-Mail Jolivia2002@yahoo.com
Sisters Touching and Agreeing Ministries
Founder and President: Olivia Thames
P.O. Box 91
Wilmington, NC 28402–0091

0-595-28379-9

Printed in the United States
47331LVS00010B/56

9 780595 283798